CONCILIUM

Religion in the Seventies

CONCILIUM

Concilium 122 (2/1979): Liturgy

STRUCTURES OF INITIATION IN CRISIS

Edited by

Luis Maldonado and David Power

THE SEABURY PRESS / NEW YORK

1979

The Seabury Press, 815 Second Avenue, New York, N.Y. 10017
ISBN: 0-8164-2230-3 (pbk.)   0-8164-0428-3

T. & T. Clark Ltd., 36 George Street, Edinburgh EH2 2LQ
ISBN: 0-567-30002-1 (pbk.)

Library of Congress Catalog Card Number: 79-65693
Printed in the United States of America

CONTENTS

Editorial

ONE OF the stray thoughts that might occur to a reader in perusing this volume on Christian initiation is that a discussion on infant baptism today would sound quite different to one that would have taken place a couple of decades ago. At that time, the ecumenical issue was whether the practice could be legitimised by an appeal to the New Testament and early Church tradition. As an internal discussion amongst Catholics the argument centred around whether or not infant baptism was a postulate of the dogma of original sin. Today, when the issue is raised, we look more to the meaning which the practice might have in a society or community and to the way that it is likely to influence the future life of the child through its relationship to the community. The question is made more complex by the realisation that the celebration does not necessarily carry univocal meaning, even within the Roman Catholic Church. Studies on popular religion have had an effect on this and similar pastoral practices, since we now know how necessary it can be to distinguish between the Church's official teaching and the expectations of pastors on the one hand, and the implications of popular belief on the other.

The discussion about Christian initiation in this volume of *Concilium* draws our attention to two points in particular, namely the reality of Christian community and the process of growth in Christian faith in the individual member. The two points are, of course, interrelated since personal growth of the individual takes place in terms of his relation to the community, its meanings, its values, its institutions, and its varied means of self-expression.

Much is written today about the number of baptised adults whose grounding in the faith is minimal and whose active participation in worship is at best seasonal. Even amongst those dubbed practising Christians there is often little community experience. When both Church and state institutions supported Christian beliefs and morals, or when Church influence was strong enough to constitute a sub-culture, such concern did not appear to be of great moment. The strong bonds of experiential face-to-face community were not vital to what was conceived to be the Christian way of life, except in those sectarian groups, usually evangelical in orientation, which separated themselves from the established churches. With the dissolution of Christian society or the waning of the Church authority's influence over its masses, the reality of Christian community becomes more problematic. Even those commentators on the current scene who protest that religious sense is as much alive as ever admit that it is often not related to ardent Church membership. This means that neither social nor religious milieu is immediately supportive of Church belonging. Consequently, the problem of Christian initiation appears in a new light.

When the Roman rite for adult initiation was published in its revised form a few years ago, it was hailed in some quarters as a promising instrument for the creation of adult faith communities. A community of personally committed adults would certainly be stronger than any body or bodies of cradle Christians whose baptism follows on birth as surely as night follows on day. It would be hasty, however, to think that we would move in a matter of years from a largescale practice of infant baptism to the common usage of adult baptism. It is probably also theologically and pastorally unsound to think that this is the only viable way of tackling the issues of adequate Christian initiation. Neither does it solve the question of what response to give to the genuine, if unsophisticated or even immature, religious sense so often present in the request for the baptism of children. It is highly important to look to the varied ways in which belonging to a community can be expressed, and to the meaning of rituals as practised, rather than to their theoretical meanings.

It emerges from a reading of the essays in this volume that the question of the age at which to celebrate the sacraments of initiation, or of the sequence in which to celebrate them, may be solved in several ways. It could be argued that not one of these ways has of necessity to be preferred to the others. In other words, different and differing pastoral approaches can be simultaneously theologically sound. As was argued in last year's *Concilium* volume on liturgy, the pastoral issue could be faced more flexibly if theologically we were less tied to a dogmatic understanding of sacramental development which is rather rigid about the number of sacraments and their respective definintions. It is not necessary to repeat that discussion here. Suffice it to say that this year's essays can help us to see that the focal point of the problem about initiation is that of personal growth within community and as member of community. In other words, we need to understand the *process* through which a person passes in coming to adult faith and identity as a member of a community of faith. We also need to investigate the meanings which the Christian symbols can have for him at the different stages of that growth.

As will appear from the articles, as well as from other writings on the subject, the term *initiation* is not now necessarily taken to indicate a moment, or even a ceremony, at which a person passes from the status of catechumen to the status of *fidelis*. A broader meaning is more often given to it which allows it to stand for the whole growth process, extending over a period of time and comprising all the factors of passage which

lead eventually to personal adult identity with the community. To discuss
initiation, therefore, is to discuss the way in which an individual, within
the appropriate context and with the appropriate support, and through
the appropriate means of induction, acquires a Christian identity which is
truly interiorised as a gift of the Lord.

Today's concern with the passage and its steps takes the personal needs
of each one, as well as the particularities of local churches, into account.
What does this passage represent in the life of an adult who moves from
non-faith to faith, or from a notional faith to faith-decision? How is it
verified in the case of a person baptised in childhood on its way through
adolescence and youth to adulthood? How much does community
belonging constitute the reality and the expression of this initiation, and
what is the appropriate nature of interaction between individual and
community? Furthermore, how does it influence the process to be born
and to grow in any given type of society? For example, what are the
differences in initiation in a community which lives in the midst of
secularised society and in one which belongs in a society where the
Catholic Church still has a dominant influence?

It follows from all these questions that in face of any proposal to
celebrate the sacraments of initiation in any particular way, the important
question is that of the meaning which such a celebration might have, given
all the individual, community and social factors involved. As already
insinuated, this implies an understanding of sacrament which is not
derived from a discussion of its effects. Meaning is constitutive of human
identity, and what is proffered through the symbols of the sacraments of
Christian initiation is that meaning which is God's gift of life in Jesus
Christ. This is not generalised and abstract meaning, but it is individuated
in proportion to the given stage of a person's life and to the environmental
conditions of the community to which it is hoped he may belong.

Some of our contributors reflect on the fact that even though the
sacramental celebration has been completed in infancy or childhood the
passage may still remain to be effected in adult life. This is most obviously
the case with those groups calling themselves *catechumenal groups,* of
which Giorgio Zevini writes. There, at least, the need has been recognised and a whole educational and ritual process is evolved to make this
passage possible. It helps not at all in such a case to affirm that the graces
of baptism have been already given in the sacrament of baptism, since it is
all too obvious that many adults have not come, or have not had the
opportunity to come, to a personal faith commitment. What is it supposed
to explain when it is affirmed that the graces are already given? That is a
purely abstract, dogmatic statement, with little relation to reality. With
infant baptism, as with any other sacramental question, it is the meaning
which the celebration can have which serves best to discern pastoral

practice. What can such a celebration seriously infuse into the life of the child through the *ekklesia's* sense and expression of Christian faith and meaning, as it bears upon the life of the child? Studies on popular religion make it clear that many nuances have to be taken into account, but this is to enlarge the question of meaning. It does not eliminate it.

Infant baptism belongs among the issues treated by several authors, but with all the nuances of today's situation placed in evidence (e.g., Nocent, Della Torre, Bourgeois, Estruch and Cardus, Blijlevens). Some authors (e.g., Della Torre, Zevini, Bourgeois, Dujarier) show how the concern shifts from such an issue to the possibilities of adult faith communities, and to adult passage from non-faith or immature faith to true and ecclesial faith decision. Where this concern exists, even questions about infant baptism have this issue primarily in mind.

The series of essays offered in the first half of the volume are intended to offer tools which the human sciences provide and which might be used towards a better understanding of all that is involved in the passage of Christian initiation (thus, Pasquier, Scheer, Berger and Lans). One of the ironies of the time is that when Christian pastoral theology has become more sensitive to passage and process and to their ritualisation, the traditional initiation programmes of societies which maintained them into the twentieth century are now falling apart. In return, however, other initiation processes, maybe less religious in significance and fostering membership in sub-cultures or interest groups are taking shape (see Pasquier). The examination to which the human sciences submit these traditional and modern initiation forms can be of help in interpreting and programming the rites and symbols of Christian initiation. As A. Nocent cautions in his article, these findings cannot be applied to Christian initiation in their brute state, but they do provide factors for our consideration. Unfortunately, in what exact way they are useful is not sufficiently probed in this volume, but that in itself may correspond rather closely to the current state of liturgical studies.

While A. Nocent's article is placed in section 1 and S. Brock's in section 2, it may be noted that these two authors approach the subject in a way which is different to that of the other contributors. They appeal more closely to the history of liturgical traditions and to the analysis of liturgical texts. This in effect serves as a compliment to the other contributions, since it means that the volume brings together three approaches to a study of liturgy: (*a*) the contemporary fact of new experiments to renew the practices of Christian initiation; (*b*) the use of the human sciences to enlighten the issues; (*c*) the lessons of history to be found in the analysis of rites and texts.

One of the chief values of a collection like this, whatever its geographical and pastoral limits, is that it allows for some sharing of experience and interest across national and linguistic boundaries. It exemplifies that plurality and diversity which now typify the liturgical scene in the Church. It is important that theological understanding and pastoral planning be rooted in the facts of the situation, whatever it be, and there can be mutual enrichment in learning how this is done in different places.

LUIS MALDONADO
DAVID POWER

PART I

Articles

Abel Pasquier

Initiation and Society

IN ORDER to describe initiation in western society,[1] we need to stand back and view it from the outside both in space and time. For how can we describe a changing process without a point of comparison to bring out the similarities and the differences? I lived for ten years in Africa south of the Sahara and was able to observe the initiation processes of the Upper Volta Mossi society.[2] When I came back to France and continued my research into initiation, I kept my African experience as a constant reference point.

Comparing Volta initiation with European sounds risky. But for me it is the best way of approaching the issue because it gives it both a synchronic and diachronic perspective: the synchronic enables us to discover beneath the multitude of forms the invariable elements that structure every initiation process; the diachronic brings out the differences in the different forms of de-structuring and re-structuring.

With this double requirement in mind I shall discuss first the Mossi, then the Western initiation processes under three headings:

the scenario or cycle of ordeals imposed;
the break with childhood or the training of desire;
the resulting integration into society.

This is merely a starting point and I cannot go into greater detail in this article. I think it gives the key to socio-cultural transmission through initiation.[3]

I. THE MOSSI OF THE UPPER VOLTA

Among the Mossi there are two initiations of the young. One, called the *poko* or 'feminisation camp', under certain conditions makes pubertal

3

girls and boys live together for a period of time which varies according to circumstances. This rite involves some of the indigenous members of the population: the 'masks', called 'sukomse'. The other rite, the *baogo*, or 'circumcision camp', involves the 'nakomse', noble foreigners from Northern Ghana who have imposed their imperial system on the country. The *baogo* lasts a shorter time, a maximum of six months for boys and less for girls, with segregation of the sexes. It is a sort of 'counter-initiation' to the sukomse and nowadays it is disintegrating faster than the *poko*.

(a) Initiatiory scenario

From the outside initiation is seen as a series of ordeals to be undergone in a certain order. The order is pre-determined and programmed in accordance with custom and great care is taken with all the stages: preparation, entry, the stay in the camp, coming out. It would take too long to describe each of these stages in detail. I shall describe only the main ordeals in the circumcision camp, which are graven upon the memories and the bodies of the candidates.

The novice undergoes the ordeal of separation: he leaves his mother and his village and is led into the bush which spirits are believed to inhabit. Here many trials await him beneath the vigilant rod of his elders. The camp begins with circumcision. During the operation, the already circumcised sing and tambourines are beaten to muffle the cries of the sufferers (some are not more than six years old) the flow of blood is staunched with dust and then the leaves of a dioecious bush are boiled and tied onto the wound. There follows a painful week called 'bitter water'. During the first three days the newly circumcised do not move but lie on the ground. They do not wash until the following Saturday when they are given the first bath which is particularly feared. The schooling in the bush is tough. The newly circumcised give up fishing, gathering plants, hunting and woodland tasks, water-carrying and thatching; they beg on the market roads. They are separated from the rest of the population and their main occupation is dancing. Every morning when they get up they are sprayed with cold water. Then they have to lie naked on their stomachs on the cold sand and they are beaten with the 'berella', to give them warmth and energy. The *baogo* discipline is harsh: violent exercise, hunger, cold, under the watchful eye of their elders who enjoy taunting them continually to make them get used to the hardship of life and obedience. To the young people this treatment is a challenge, a passage from fear of suffering and death to the acceptance of risk. This requires a personal commitment. Being a spectator is not enough. Society only accepts strong men, conquering heroes, especially in its knights who are 'ouedraogo' ('male horses'), thorough-bred stallions capable of fending off all enemies. The water of the bath of circumcision, the painful bath with a wound that still stings and burns, is water that mortifies, water that kills. The whole stay in the camp is made up of violations of childhood prohibitions, but in return unconditional obedience to the fathers' laws is required. They come out of the bush as if it were the Marigot, a river, or the mother's womb: with violent pushes, tearing the amniotic sack and swimming. This is the only way to become hardened and be born into the world of grown men.

(b) The break with childhood

Initiation marks the necessary adolescent passage from childhood confusion to the 'splitting' of the sexes. At the appropriate time the adults customarily enforce upon the young the separation necessary to their emotional maturing and introduce them into a world of insecurity after their period of maternal and family warmth. The various ordeals are stages in a training process in which the education of desire has a paramount role.

The *poko* of the masks, which I now describe, is a mixed initiation; it takes place at the death of the 'master of the earth'.[4] Pubertal boys and girls go through it together for three, six or nine years, according to the length of the reign of the dead man. Let us examine how desire is trained in these conditions.

At the beginning of his life the small native child experiences a phase of intense pleasure which leaves an indelible mark upon him. He is joined to his mother like a parasite, is carried everywhere by her on her back, and finds it difficult to conceive of himself apart from her; thus the cutting of the umbilical cord is, as it were, delayed, and the (born) baby continues for a long time to live a foetal-like life. He is never separated from his mother and his every instinct is immediately satisfied. Later a break becomes necessary. The gourd must be broken and the stalk joining the fruit to the tree cut. The bitter law of separation cuts like a sharp knife. It is a critical period for the child's health. It leaves a painful memory and he feels like an abandoned orphan ill-treated by a wicked stepmother.

He is in fact completely orphaned at the beginning of the *poko*. The young man is torn away from the maternal feminine sphere and the young girl must enter a feminine world outside the parental orbit. The time for being fused with the mother is over. Now they must learn control, self-restraint and self mastery. Going out into the bush feels like dying: a symbolic death to enter into fuller life, and initiatory death which is more a new beginning than an end. Many prohibitions are imposed upon the novices in mixed groups. The prohibitions against wearing clothes and ornaments is concerned with sexual relationships. One of the greatest faults that can be committed in *poko* is for a boy to 'show off his male beauty' and for a girl to play the flirt. This demand is imposed because the young people of both sexes live in close quarters. During their whole stay in camp they are always naked in their huts and when they go out, until the day they are permitted to wear a loin cloth of animal skin—the nakedness of the child still attached to its mother, a state of innocence regained by hard self-denial.

Self-mastery is not the only requirement for becoming a man or a woman. By means of nine principal festivals the novices are trained to live in accordance with the system of inter-personal relationships ordained by the culture. Most of these festivals concentrate on a particular form of social relationship. Everything is carefully programmed: the invitation of masks from neighbouring villages, the entertainment of the people from the native village, the festival for mothers and maternal aunts, the visit by the bridegroom to his promised bride in the camp, celebrations of friendship between male and female partners: on one day the boys entertain, on another the girls. Anyone who does not accept the social system, and is incapable of heterosexual friendship cannot be a good husband or wife. Emotional warmth which was formerly confined to blood relations expands towards others. Everyone is made to understand that sexuality in all its ramifications is a matter for group concern, not just individuals. The *poko* atmosphere is quite different from the aristocratic *baogo* which is influenced by Islam. Identification with the world of adult men or adult women, the overcoming of the Oedipus problem is a task facing all alike. The two ethnic classes in the Mossi each have their own methods. Only at the end of this long exercise are the boys and girls mature enough to fulfil their functions as men and women.

(c) Reintegration into society

Initiation is a change of state. It restructures the relationships between the generations and introduces a newly adult group into society. The Mossi boy can walk out proudly from the circumcision camp because he has become a man. He makes a point of parading himself in the market. He dresses up in finery and goes about with other adults to display his re-entry into public life. This is a great day for him which he will remember long. 'They are real men, real males!' the villagers whisper admiringly when the newly initiated return from camp, because now these boys are mature enough to be real links in the chain of generations. This is the result of the Volta initiation process; it is a system for reproducing social relationships which are apparently the same as they have always been. The institution works by means of its constant reference to the same foundation myth. The Mossi are a society in which initiation has a predominant role supported by a ritual training based on an original myth passed down from generation to generation.

1. The foundation myth

This is a folk tale which explains in symbolic terms the origin of life through the separation of sky and earth. In the story a blind man lit a torch which burnt the sky so that it drew back forever. This story tells the ultimate meaning of life, by referring back to 'in illo tempore', the matrix of all times, the beginning when institutions and prerogatives of age, sex, power and knowledge were set up. This is the nucleus of the Mossi vision not only of the cosmos but of the whole socio-cultural system. The original opposition between sky and earth (cosmos) is analogous to that between man and woman (sex), which corresponds to a third: foreigner and native (social class) and so on throughout all possible dualities such as *baogo/poko* (initiation), salt/tamarind tree (trade), horse/donkey (mount), stick/gourd (utensils), sun cult/earth cult, exorcism/ identification with spirits. At all levels of the socio-cultural system we find these pairs of opposites defining a dualistic conception of the world and providing a way of coping with the tensions inherent in human life. The foundation myth gives the Mossi world its structure and impeccable coherence.

2. Ritual training

Both instruction and apprenticeship are contained in the initiation process. This does not mean that they only take place there; they also take place in the family, for example. But the initiation process is their culmination. The key to the Mossi initiation process is, we repeat, its constant reference to the original myth; the rites merely celebrate and put into effect what was done once and for all. The novices are progressively metamorphosed in the image of the clan's eponymous ancestor, and symbolically relive his act, which was the foundation of all knowledge and all action.

I do not think we can really speak of instruction by means of abstract concepts or precise formulations here. The process is a diffuse handing down, through experience rather than thinking, of a tradition descernible through the liturgical rites employed. The materials used represent the symbolic capital of the tribe: objects, gestures, words, are always exactly the same in life's main celebrations: birth, naming, separation, marriage, first pregnancy and funeral. From his youth, by means of these rites the novice becomes familiar with the great themes which dominate his thinking. The point is not to verbalise them but to make them come alive.

The same goes for apprenticeship. The neophyte is truly re-born and has to re-learn how to live, walk, eat, speak and hoe . . . to behave properly as custom requires (*doogem-mikri* = 'what you find when you are born'). Things which were previously an occasional apprenticeship are re-communicated in a stereotyped manner with appropriate rules and secrets. The secrets are only passed on to those who have shown themselves worthy by their efforts and the strength of their desire to identify with the tribal ancestor.

II. MODERN WESTERN SOCIETY

The context has changed radically.[5] The first obvious observation is that western society no longer has an initiation process. There are no longer any special institutions for 'rites of passage' for the young to adulthood. Family, school and church, which used to perform these functions, have lost their authority and are less and less sure of their capacity to guide their young through the stages of growing up and becoming members of adult society. Yet the initiation process of former centuries are deeply embedded in the culture and may spring up again, without our realising it, under new forms. Here I discuss only the initiatory phenomena which concern the young, according to my recent observations. I shall use the same model as I used for the Mossi.[6]

(a) Scenario

At first sight the initiation process seems to have collapsed into chaos with bits and pieces of it observable in all sorts of places. This shows at least that it is still going on in some way or another in our society.

1. Revival of initiatory elements in the contemporary imagination

The symbolism of the initiation process comes from an original pattern which is found in all cultures. The ancient myths upon which initiation is based all have the same invariable elements. Jung invented a term to describe this phenomenon: the archetype. There is a prototype of initiation in the collective memory of all peoples, but it is expressed in different ways. The Mossi stories of the orphan can be used to discover the dynamics of the two initiations they bear witness to. The Celtic tales of the Glass Castle or the Journeys to the Sun which my godmother told me no doubt refer to long forgotten initiations. These folk tales, whether Mossi or Indo-European, were passed down from generation to generation. This is no longer the case in a world where the initiatory process is projected towards the science fiction future hailing the advent of 'mutants'. Why this trend? Could it be because there is something lacking in the real world, and so science fiction appeals to some essential need in ourselves we have difficulty in fulfilling?

2. Initiatory experiences among the young

When the adult world is in crisis, the young dream dreams. The re-emergence of the initiatory archetype in our literary and audio-visual culture, does not appear to be a hallucinatory refusal to face reality; it is a sign that the whole society is breaking with the past. The initiatory processes or their substitutes no longer have any social symbolism in which they can be expressed and are at odds with the established system. So they surreptitiously seek other ways and break out violently in them. The young are frustrated with institutions they can no longer believe in and look elsewhere. They are the first to seek new experiences in which initiatory ordeals are not absent. Analysing about thirty accounts of young people relating their experiences, I realise that the cycle of initiatory ordeals could be found in movements as different as the local gang, the drug culture, journeys, small communities, sex-segrated groups, political splinter groups, group therapy sessions etc.

We can surely speak of ordeals in all these cases. However, we should note one new characteristic as compared with Volta initiations. Although these new scenes are initiatory, the methods used are techniques and thus can be compared to apprenticeship. Drug takers, for example, 'take-off' by using chemical means of the pharmaceutical civilisation they have rejected.

In most of the accounts I was given, the ordeal is supposed to be a 'short-cut' to achieve the desired goal as quickly as possible. The avowed aim is a transformation of the self and its relationships to others and the world. It is expressed in terms of transmutation, which is more like an alchemical process than an initiation process because the latter respects the slow and gradual growth of the personality.

(b) The break with childhood

Traditional initiatory processes gave symbolic means of access to the status of adulthood in society. The development of desire was an important part of the process. Today there is the same need for the human being to change state and to escape from everyday routine. The same emotional growth process is necessary to the balance in the relationships between generations and between the sexes. Every human being in every culture, by virtue of his or her sexual nature, is drawn to seek another by recognising a fundamental lack in him/herself. Our very natures suffer from this radical incompleteness all our lives. We seek the other, from whom we are cut off (by 'secateurs', sex), and our search is never fulfilled. Neither are we able to remain in a state of autism, the inability ever to emerge from the primitive satisfaction which prevents us from learning to speak and communicate with others.

1. Enclosure within the self

This is the attitude of drug takers as in this unpublished manuscript which is an extract from a fictional autobiography: 'What was happening to me? My heart was gone and my body languished. I did not want it to be so, but my body was inert and defenceless. I resisted mentally but my body floated away from me into darkness. I drank and took drugs. I took the boy and he took me. There was a hideous duality running through my body, I retched, I felt completely defeated and lost all notion of time and space. So where was I? I was hungry and thirsty for love. I was just a tiny point on the human horizon, diminishing.' 'I took', 'he took', a mirror image in which the otherness of the partner is not recognised. The other is only the expansion, the image of myself. So it is not surprising if 'I' become a 'little girl' again, I dissolve like a small point on the horizon.

In some cases, these small communities who are trying to create a life-style free from paternity and the institution of the family, return to a state of savagery. In Laplantine's phrase they live in a state of permanent 'social orgasm', a tribal life, which finds only the bitterness of being enclosed within the self.[7]

2. The rejection of prohibitions

By their failures young people come to realise that limitless enjoyment does not exist. The prohibition basic to any social group cannot be denied. A new race cannot arise without it.[8] In sex 'the magic of love' is absolute. At the climax 'the man is annihilated by the exhaustive giving of his substance and the woman rocks in unconsciousness as if she were dead: this is the divine orgasm.[9] Self-restraint to break with childhood is abandoned. Priority is given to the immediate moment. However the immediate moment cannot break free of what history has wrought in both people and things.

3. Self-initiation

One characteristic deriving from the above-mentioned attitudes, which prevents certain experiences from being initiatory, is that these experiences are self-conscious and aware of the mechanisms involved. The drug taker seeks euphoria by taking marijuana or grass and getting high, and an increase of intellectual perception by taking heroin. This is a kind of self-initiation which cannot function properly, because initiation functions by the use of symbols. In many accounts of drug taking[10] we find no image or metaphor capable of sustaining the dynamics of desire but operational concepts and rationalisations.[11]

The stress is on what is felt, the quasi-sensual encounter with the self and the other; priority is given to experience, feeling. You 'feel yourself', you 'explode'. This means that the intellect is left aside. Rogers speaks of the 'necessity of feeling oneself to be a process of personalities'. No doubt this is true, but isn't the price too high? Sometimes this way madness lies. Then symbols take over again, but they are uncontrolled and defy any attempt to make a coherent pattern of them.[12]

(c) Social Integration

Whereas traditional initiation led the young to take responsibility in the adult institutions of their society, and to work vigorously with their new strength, modern western initiatory phenomena seem to be working in the opposite direction.

1. Rejection

All the experiences described above are attempts to challenge the established system. They appeal to the subversive power of initiatory elements to encourage other ways of living. They all reject integration into established society. They reject the primacy of the work ethic, the male, money, authority, received knowledge, technical progress, political projects.

The 'situationist' movement in particular, rejects the system absolutely and proposes a general strike from work and even from procreation. This revolt is a desire to return to primal chaos and it hopes for something outside or beyond existing institutions.

2. Enclosure

The young 'keep themselves to themselves', in sects of a more or less odd nature. They are accessible only to the initiates. Group therapy is practised in a closed place, outside the ordinary framework of life. This is even a necessary condition for its effectiveness, which is limited to its own enclosed area of operations. Neither before nor after matters. The neophyte is perhaps reborn, to face life anew, but he then has to go on to do everything for himself, beginning with the leaving of this artificial micro-society and facing other people in everyday life.

3. A new renaissance

Looking ahead, perhaps we might wonder whether these pseudo-initiations are the first signs of a mutation in western society. At least they are exploring counter-systems. Their deliberate attempt to invert existing processes, without as yet offering successful alternatives, at least expresses the need for social structures better adapted to our present technological environment. Who can foresee the outcome?

CONCLUSION

Of course the ethnographer should not risk playing at prophecy. I simply want to make three observations, of the truth of which I have become firmly convinced.

1. Mossi society favoured an initiation process whereas western society is dominated by the technical apprenticeship process. This means that initiation processes cannot be described in a 'pure state'. They have to be seen in the total context of the culture in which they function and of the various educational and apprenticeship devices they use. The three fundamental elements in socio-cultural transmission must be constantly pulled apart and re-combined according to the needs of the society.

2. Initiation can be either a process of reproducing or subverting an established system.[13] This means that the development of societies does not depend solely on changes in power and structure as institutional analysis claims.[14]

3. I think the most crucial thing is the training of desire undertaken or made possible by the existing institutions. The work of renewal must be done step by step, in daily life through modest but constant efforts. In this process, the retention of prohibition has a fundamental part to play.

Translated by Dinah Livingstone

Notes

1. This article is derived from a larger work which is part of the 'Parcours Intensifs de l'Extension Universitaire de l'Institut Catholique'. Two study groups have contributed greatly to it: 'Savoir, apprentissage, initiation' (J. Audinet, O. Dubuisson, A. Pasquier) for the study of socio-cultural transmission on a worldwide scale, and 'Adolescence: initiation, pédagogie' for initiation (P. Mayol, A. Pasquier).

2. A. Pasquier *Initiations au Moogo et contes de l'orphelin,* sociology thesis at Descartes University, Paris, 1976.

3. The basic elements in this problem are discussed by J. Audinet and A. Pasquier 'Pratique du langage, culture et foi' in *Langages et Cultures* (Paris 1978) pp. 127-46.

4. Person customarily in charge of the ownership of land and the cult of the earth.

5. Of course I cannot give an account here of all the initiatory phenomena in western European society and their cultural differences according to country or

even region. My study is limited to a first approach to the young, particularly in the Paris region.

6. A. Pasquier *Approche Ethnolinguistique d'un Conte Moose, Mémoire de Diplome des Hautes Etudes* (Paris 1976). In this I explain my methods of analysis, which I have also followed in my study of the texts about western youth. These texts have been taken chiefly from: A. Bercoff, N. Devil, P. Salomon, *Nu, le Livre des Possibilitiés* (Paris 1977).

Collective: *Almanach Actuel 1978* published by the periodical *Actuel* (Paris 1977); 'Dix années sacrileges' *Autrement* (Paris 1978).

7. See A. Bercoff *op. cit.* p. 220.

8. See *Almanach op. cit.* pp. 141-2.

9. M. Rouet *La Magie de l'Amour.* I have read no. 0102 (Paris 1978) p. 252.

10. See A. Bercoff *op. cit.* p. 220.

11. *Ibid.* p. 264.

12. *Ibid.* p. 92.

13. Besides the phenomena I have criticised, there are others which may represent a *third way* and seem to be a genuine re-discovery of initiation. Among those I have come across, I should like to mention the 'communes', certain noviciates, 'youth camps', spiritual retreat centres, school councils, residents' associations, groups for welcoming immigrants.

14. In fact the fundamental relationship in society is not that between dominators and dominated. Power like knowledge is exercised within a system of a number of basic relationships: sexual (men/women), generation (parents/children, older and younger, peer groups), territory (natives/foreigners). The initiation process must take account of all these polarities.

Anthonius Scheer

The Influence of Culture on the Liturgy as shown in the History of the Christian Initiation Rite

IN RECENT years a number of important studies on Christian initiation has appeared in the field of liturgiology. This seems to indicate that people want to re-assess their understanding of the basis and the implied commitment of Christian life. This initiation, indeed, formally introduces a person into the faith both as an individual and as the member of a community. But the various questions about initiation can be looked at from different angles: that of systematic theology, comparative religion, anthropology, pastoral theology, exegesis, the history of liturgy, and so on, and all these approaches can, in turn, again be narrowed down to one or other particular issue. At present it is simply impossible to produce a fully comprehensive study of initiation as a whole, and this only shows the complexity of the problem as it appears today.

In this article I have concentrated on the historical angle because it is in this field of history that at present some rather searching questions are being put regarding initiation. I am convinced that the results of historical research are vital for any other approach to the problem. I do not intend to further this historical research on any particular point but rather to report on the results achieved so far. Here I want to concentrate on the way culture influenced liturgical actions in the initiation rite in the past, and obviously only a few themes can be dealt with in this article.[1]

THE WAY IN WHICH THE PAST HAS CONDITIONED THE PRESENT

There are three clusters of issues which I shall not deal with in this discussion. They are the specifically ecumenical questions concerning baptism today,[2] questions about the relation between baptism and confirmation,[3] and the questions relating to infant baptism and the baptism of adults. It is not that these questions are not very important, but here I see them as a legacy from the past which originated in times when the main shape of the liturgy had already been more or less fixed. One may, for instance, well ask whether we would still have to cope with this kind of problem today if in the past the actual shaping of the liturgy had proceeded on other lines. This may sound like a peculiar observation but it is a fact that the situation of initiation is still far less complex in the Eastern Churches than in the West.

From early on the Eastern Churches were accustomed to ritual diversity among the various liturgical traditions which, as such, did not conflict with each other. They do not know the ritual separation between what in the West came to be called baptism and confirmation because there, both these elements are part of one liturgical action. At an early date they found ways of giving infant baptism a ritual expression of its own which maintained features of the classical initiation liturgy in the post-Constantinian period but displayed considerable adaptation to the practice of infant baptism.[4]

Against this background of the Eastern situation one may well be surprised at the following aspects of the Western tradition: 1. that up till recently the Catholic and the Protestant Churches criticised each other's administration of baptism[5]; 2. that until recently the Catholic Church imposed a uniform initiation rite wherever the Church found itself; 3. that only in our own generation has the Catholic Church formulated a special rite for infant baptism[6]; 4. that Catholicism still continues to make a fundamental distinction between the sacraments of baptism and confirmation although both constitute one single initiation.[7] All this raises today some basic questions which, however, are very much conditioned by history. What the student of the history of the liturgy is quite clear about is that the situation which has developed in the West with regard to the initiation rite should not be blamed on Providence but seen as largely brought about by cultural factors and influences. In other words, there are plenty of socio- and psycho-cultural arguments to explain not only this development but also the theological, particularly the scholastic, discussion which followed it. And so we come to the real question of this article: How far have the origin and development of the Christian initiation liturgy been determined by culture?

In listing a number of findings produced by the study of the history of liturgy I shall work backward in time, starting from the early middle ages.

1. *The early medieval situation in the West: the consolidation of the past*

The most important sources of the Western liturgy date from the sixth and seventh centuries and later.[8] These show, first of all, an archaising and conservative idea of Christian worship. At that time initiation was in practice no longer a matter of baptising adults. The catechumenate, handed down with its ritual, had become a formula recalling the past. It was mainly children who were initiated. The more one thinks about this situation, the more one is struck by the fact that the documents of this period are almost wholly detached from actuality. Practically all the texts and rubrics still seem to take for granted that initiation is an adult affair. Of the factors which may have assisted this process I mention only two.

First of all, the concept of original sin was expanded in the West as a typical legacy of the Pelagian controversy and it was applied to the new-born infant with all its detailed implications. It is indeed curious that only one traditional part was further developed in the ritual, namely, the 'scrutiny' in the sense of the solemn exorcism of the devil. As I see it, this means that in those days the doctrine of original sin so dominated the cultural life of the faith that it had repercussions on the initiation rite in an age when baptism was mainly administered to children. This is a good illustration of how theology—which had by then become common property—could affect liturgical practice.

The second factor may be described as the way in which memories of the good old days were kept alive. The early medieval manuscripts show that at that time the main preoccupation was concerned with passing on what had already become custom. When the liturgy of adult catechumens was still actual and meaningful, the *traditio* and *redditio symboli* was considered an important ceremony in the rite of the conversion of an adult. But what can such a ceremony possibly mean in the case of an infant? The infant is not yet capable of truly accepting or returning anything. The most that can be done is that the godparents go through the ceremony in his stead. But what happened? Instead of leaving such ceremonies out or replacing them, the Western Church actually inflated them. In the documents we not only read about the performing of the *traditio symboli* in both Greek and Latin, but the infant has also to bear with the recitation of the four gospels and the Our Father.

I can only interpret this development as follows. What people know and appreciate from the past they like to have carefully preserved and even reinforced, even if a changed situation has made it all irrelevant. The result of this has been that the rites meant for adult catechumens and no longer applicable were neither dropped nor replaced but expanded instead. This explains how and why the ritual of infant baptism became futile in the West. But this early medieval practice appears to have been mainly determined, and in fact even restricted, by the *culture* of the living faith, prevailing at that time, with far-reaching consequences for the initiation liturgy in the West.

2. *The period after Constantine: the past brought into the present*

There is plenty of information about the initiation liturgy during the patristic age (fourth-sixth century). This information can be gathered from the mystagogical catecheses of such great figures as Ambrose, Cyril of Jerusalem, John Chrysostom and Theodore of Mopsuestia,[9] the homilies of St Augustine[10] and Asterius the Sophist,[11] and such liturgical texts as the *Constitutiones Apostolorum*.[12] This was the peak period for the initiation liturgy. When Constantine changed the course of the Roman Empire, the Christian communities discovered they were officially recognised and free. So there was an influx of applicants who had to pass through the initiation system. In the changed political climate realists decided it made sense to belong to a Christian community. From the point of view of the Christians one might describe this as the emancipatory effect of the peace of Constantine. The community became a public institution, just as recognisable as the former state religion with its institutions. It showed itself openly in persons, buildings, all kinds of artistic development, literature, and so on. The position of the pedagogue and the philosopher in the past was gradually taken over by the catechist and the mystagogue. It is really very important to realise that during this period the Christian communities had the God-given opportunity to develop total acculturisation—an opportunity which, so far, has never occurred again. One of the areas in which this acculturation took shape was the initiation liturgy.

On the basis of the mystical catecheses in particular one realises that this period was specially concerned with bringing about some kind of harmony between the initiation rites and the contemporary way of life. After all, the considerable groups of adults who turned to the Church came from a pagan Hellenistic environment. The Church therefore had to try to bridge the gap between the old and the new. In practice this was done through initiation rites, adjusted to the culture of the age on the one hand, but stressing the biblical message, particularly the pascha of the Lord, on the other. Great use was made of Paul's theology of baptism in Romans 6. The data of this period create the impression that the various local churches, such as Jerusalem, Antioch, Milan and Hippo, did not aim at general uniformity in the initiation rites. On the contrary, many local customs went through a phase of development with the already trad- itional initiation ritual as its starting-point. It was a period of liturgical growth and change.[13]

There are two points which we ought to mention in the context of this article. The idea of having an initiation liturgy at all is for a large part to bring about a new orientation of life in a deeper understanding of the world one lives in. This is why the rites and their meaning had to be worked out in a way which was culturally acceptable. So the baptismal rite (in the narrow sense) was linked with the bathing habits of the time, the anointing rites with the anointing customs in the thermae, in sport and medical practice, the signing or marking rites with the ways in which animals, soldiers and domestic servants were branded or marked. The rites used for catechumens were clarified by linking them with social and culturally conditioned customs: kneeling and rising, turning round, stretching one's arms towards heaven, turning one's face eastward or westward, rejecting with a gesture of the hand, seeing the font, undressing and dressing, descending into and rising from the font. All this shows that the idea was to drive home and reinforce the way in which the liturgical ceremonies harmonised with the surrounding cultural habits. So the initiation ritual adopted during this period actions and gestures to which people were already accustomed through their ordinary behaviour. Every local church seems to have gone its own way here and the churches may have been influenced by each other. In simple words, the ritual shape of the initiation was largely influenced by contemporary culture and behaviour while, on its part, it also deepened the meaning of this cultural behaviour. So there was a willingness to bring about a viable relationship between the life of faith and life *tout court*.

Another relevant fact is that theological thinking about the ritual was also conditioned by the spirit of the age. Here I really mean the vast influence of St Paul's theology of baptism in this period. The various factors which led to this were: 1. the great prestige of Paul's letters among Hellenistic Christians at that time; 2. the memorable character of the way in which worship was presented through the typological exegesis of baptism as well as of the eucharist; 3. the central place taken by the pascha of the Lord as a whole, including passion, death, resurrection and ascension, as the core of the Christian economy of salvation; 4. the way in which the baptismal rite had in the meantime found expression in either immersion or submersion which corresponded to Paul's idea of dying, being buried and rising with the Lord in a concrete gesture, and perhaps, 5. the more or less conscious way in which pagan initiation rites related to the dying of the god as brought out in these pagan rites.[14] With these complex elements the catechists and mystagogues of the period in question worked out a ritual which could be understood and make the faith acceptable. In this way the ritual showed a definite aptness while maintaining an explicit and lively interest in the bible.

3. *The first Christian centuries: sorting out the Christian attitude towards the surrounding culture*

When we turn to the first Christian centuries our information is rather limited. The main evidence is contained in writings from Syria (the *Didascalia Apostolorum*), Rome (Hippolytus), Africa (Tertullian and Cyprian) and Egypt (Clement and Origen). From the initiation ritual of Hippolytus[15] one gathers that joining the community entailed social conditions concerning labour, profession and marriage which the candidate had to satisfy. The candidate's way of life was examined in some detail. He was exorcised by imposition of hands and prayer. He had to abjure the past: Satan with all his pomps and works. The community was clearly aware of its hostile environment. It explicitly rejected the culture current in society and looked at it critically. It saw itself as a small select group of high spiritual calibre. It was fully aware of its identity with regard to the religious situation outside. Its initiation procedure must be seen in the light of this attitude. This whole treatment of the candidate indicates the community's critical approach to its pagan environment in order to ensure a true conversion to the God of Jesus of Nazareth and to protect its own internal life. The solid structure of Hippolytus' community made it strong with regard to the world in which it lived.

But there is still another striking element in his initiation ritual. This is the rich outgrowth of the post-baptismal rites of anointing and the imposition of hands. In this connection one must also mention his African contemporary, Tertullian with his typical distinction between the baptism with water and the imposition of hands. This made him even speak of 'two sacraments'.[16] Apart from this there is also a number of Syrian texts[17] where the pre-baptismal anointing is explicitly linked with the gift of the Spirit. In other words, this period already knows a differentiation within the basic structure of the initiation rite. How should one explain this? From the historical point of view it is maintained that the rite was influenced by the Stoicism and gnosticism of contemporary Hellenism. In his teaching about the Spirit, Tertullian borrowed ideas from Stoicism with the help of which he explained that water-rite brought about the likeness with God while the imposition of hands conveyed the gift of the Spirit. The Syrian writings which attributed great value to 'marking' or 'signing' through anointing show the influence of gnostic circles where people liked to see initiation as the seal, imprinted on the believer and marking him out for the 'spiritual life', through which he renounced material values and turned away from the evil influence of dark spiritual powers.[18] To express these ideas in a ceremony they turned by preference to anointing as signifying the gift of the Spirit through which one became a member of the pneumatic circle.

During this period the initiation ritual appears to have been influenced by various intellectual trends which, in a basic way, determined the choice and the shape of the Christian ritual. So we see here again that the surrounding society helped the Christian community to develop its own outlook and that it expressed this outlook appropriately in its liturgical worship as illustrated in the case of the initiation rite. But this inevitably brings up the question of the basic structure of Christian initiation.

4. *The Beginnings*

How did the Christian communities of the first century cope with the initiation as it was seen at the start? Was it seen as something totally original to Christianity or as something which had its roots in contemporary culture? It is not exactly a simple matter to convey the problems connected with the origin of the baptismal ritual. But, at present, the historical study of the initiation ritual seems to concentrate on the origins.[19] First of all, it is accepted that the original rite was very simple. This is evidenced by the New Testament, the *Didachè* and the *Acta Thomae*. At that time the basic elements were the waterbath, the imposition of hands, the anointing and confessing to the Lord or the triune God.[20] In this connection, the following observations have been made. 1. The water rite, universally attested, seems to have had no connections with the bathing habits of the time, nor with the baptism of Jewish proselytes, nor directly with such ritual washings as took place in the Qumran community. But a link with John's baptism is accepted because of its 'once-for-all' character, its eschatological summons to all the people and the administration of it by the Baptist himself.[21] 2. It seems more or less certain that the water rite did not consist of immersion; it was composed of stepping into the water, the pouring of water over the head of the candidate by whoever administered the baptism, accompanied by the confession of the Name, and followed by stepping out of the water.[22] 3. The trinitarian formula of Mt. 28:19, Mk. 16:18 and Didachè 7:1-3 is seen as having developed from the original christological one: this latter is taken as having originated among the Judaeo-Christians of Palestine who were converted 'to the Lord', while the former probably arose among the Syrian pagan converts who were asked to confess 'the God of the Christians'. 4. At first people were baptised in 'living', i.e., naturally flowing water but later on this was given a broader interpretation in order to meet local conditions (*Did.* in Syria).[23] It was also in Syria that we meet the first mention of a pre-baptismal anointing (*Acta Thomae*).[24] 5. In so far as the original structure of the initiation is concerned, modern research tends to accept the hypothesis that the first communities baptised mainly by bathing in water, but because this simple explanation fails to cover all the New Testament data (Acts 8:17; 19:6; 9:17; 10:44-48; 1 Cor. 10:1-2; 1 John 5:8; Heb. 6:2) and those of the post-apostolic age (*Didachè, Acta Thomae*), scholars accept the possibility that the apostolic age already knew of different initiation rites which had some connection with the religio-cultural background of the converts.[25] According to this view the Palestinian Christians would have followed the tradition of John the Baptist; in the diaspora they would have continued the tradition of the Jewish proselytes; some charismatic circles would have continued the rabbinic rite of the imposition of hands signifying the gift of the Spirit, while communities influenced by gnostic ideas stressed the 'signing' or 'marking' rites through the ritual anointing.

Research into the original forms of Christian initiation is still far from complete. At present it appears to be accepted that, whatever form the ritual took, there was a link with the religious and cultural background of these Christians. It is also accepted that we should first look at the traditions which were already existing within Judaism when Christianity began to take wing. The pluriform way in which converts influenced the original communities obviously meant that there were various ways of performing the initiation. These original communities expressed the new and irreducible element in Christian initiation in various ways in order to meet the needs and understanding of those that came new to their own situation.

5. *Summing up*

This too summary and generalised survey of the main phases in the development of the initiation liturgy is meant to show principally how culture influenced the origin and development of the rites which composed it. It leads, however, to the conclusion that the Christian way of performing its liturgical worship was influenced by the surrounding culture, and not only at every stage, but also in the way it was interpreted by the theologians. The historical investigation of these initiation rites indicates that they were freely determined by the existing culture. This means that there were constantly new and viable cultural elements which the Christian communities accepted and used to give expression to the way in which these communities saw salvation. This general conclusion based on historical research cannot be reconciled with the idea that Christian initiation was a totally original product, coming out of the blue, at whatever stage, a product to be attributed to some direct institutional act of the Lord or any of his first disciples.

THE IMPOSSIBILITY OF DIVORCING CULTURE FROM LITURGICAL WORSHIP

We have never felt at ease with the idea that culture determined Christian liturgy even at its origin and in its basic structures. We have indeed been thoroughly conditioned by the approach of classical theology and as a result we have looked upon the core of these rites as being such an originally and exclusively Christian feature that they could only be seen as directly instituted by the Lord or his immediate company. This view no doubt expresses one aspect of the problem. It is the result of a living faith looking at the essence of Christian worship. But this one-sided emphasis practically prevented the Western tradition from recognising that Christian worship was also essentially conditioned by, and situated in, history. This may be even more true for the Prostestant Churches than for Catholicism. But, when taking a serious look at worship and liturgy, should we not at the outset face the fact that this liturgical worship was shaped by two components of equal value, faith and culture, a point of view confirmed by historical research? These two components joined in moulding one symbolic reality in a way which preserved the visible and experiential identity of each. It is indeed of the essence of liturgical worship that it is both genuine as an expression of the faith and alive as an expression of contemporary culture. Neglecting this dialectic of liturgical worship simply leads to a kind of monophysitism. The history of the initiation ritual shows that in the long run the balance was weighted in favour of neo-chalcedonism.

When we think about the nature of Christian liturgy we always end up with the eternal problem of the relation between nature and grace, world and faith, God and man. But it is important to realise that if we formulate the dilemma like this we are almost forced to sacrifice one to the other. This is a permanent temptation within the Christian movement which has regularly felt itself bound to oppose what is human and this-worldly. The clearest evidence for this can be found in the history of the Western liturgy. This shows that in the West Christendom built up its liturgy to such a pitch of stable and model expression of the sacral in Christianity that again and again, and in whatever situation, it closed the door on any culture within which it was meant to live. The initiation ritual is a striking example of this.

When we apply this dilemma of nature and grace to the liturgy there is no simple and straightforward solution. Both nature and grace remain abstractions unless embodied in a concrete situation. But this is imposs- ible without the human and the 'this-worldly' element. One might call this the permanent incarnational aspect of the liturgy as it inserts grace into nature. In this light we see the human and worldly aspects of life as open to grace. But this is not the whole answer to the problem since worship not only conveys divine realities—it also is a *manifestation* of them. The form of the liturgy must show, express and convey the divine reality. This is one of the reasons why it is essential that the Christian movement must be able to discover in its actual situation elements which, because of their inner and outward meaningfulness, lend themselves to the conveying and manifesting of grace, incarnation and epiphany. This is where the pluriformity of culture find its concrete expression. Perhaps we may even say that culture essentially demands to be completed in a *cultus*. The 'future' contained in the potential of culture (*cultura*) will again and again insist on being achieved in the 'perfect' (*cultus*). Up to a point we saw this in the history of the initiation liturgy, particularly during the first centuries.

SOME OBSERVATIONS ABOUT PASTORAL THEOLOGY

1. The significance of culture for religious worship should be taken seriously and thought out with some logical consistency. If this is done, it will have an important effect not only on the liturgical conduct and attitude of the community but also on the way in which the liturgy is treated in preaching and religious instruction. Our present situation requires that both the ideas about liturgy and its concrete expression be adjusted to the surrounding culture in a systematic way and without restriction. This holds for the young churches as well as for the old ones. The latter particularly should overcome the peculiar difficulties which now beset them because this development has been put off for centuries.

2. This fundamental adjustment of liturgical worship to its surrounding culture is today a pastoral task which can no longer be avoided. For this the clergy need the ability to observe and to discern as well as good taste. Without these qualities they would not be able to discover within their actual cultural environment the kind of values, elements, words and actions which can lend themselves to interpretation and integration in terms of liturgical worship. Anyone looking for this is surrounded by people and communities, and from his observation post among them can point out where, how, and in what way these people and communities most truly recognise themselves.

3. The general introduction to the Roman *ordines* for infant and adult baptism contains the following statement (n. 31): 'Given the declarations made in the Constitution on the Liturgy (art. 37-40 and 65) the Episcopal Conferences in missionary regions must see whether the various peoples have elements in their initiation practices which could be adapted or used in the Christian rite of baptism. They can decide according to their own

judgement.' This text refers to a few basic pronouncements of Vatican II on the subject of liturgical renewal in general. Here it is a matter of adapting elements of some existing initiation practice and their insertion into the Roman ritual. To this may be added what is said in n. 30 *sub* 2: (the Episcopal Conference should) 'examine with care and the necessary prudence what can be taken over from the native character and traditions of the peoples and other adaptations which are useful or necessary, submit these to the Holy See, and introduce them after having obtained approval'. Here it is a matter of taking over elements from the native character and traditions of indigenous peoples in order to bring the Roman ritual up to date. In fact the new liturgical laws were intended to internationalise the fundamental structure and basic elements of the Roman ritual in a no doubt suitable way in order to preserve the unity of the Western liturgy. Compared with the Roman Ritual as it was, the new Roman *ordines* show that there has been a renewal on many points. Yet, it is all still so much on the lines of the past that it is difficult to see there any real opportunity for a genuine acculturation of the Christian initiation ritual.

Translated by Theo Weston

Notes

1. Meaningful historical surveys can be found in B. Neunheuser 'Taufe und Firmung' (*Handbuch der Dogmengeschichte* IV, 2 (Freiburg 1958)); A. Stenzel *Die Taufe. Eine genetische Erklärung der Taufliturgie* (Innsbruck 1958); G. R. Beasley-Murray, *Baptism in the New Testament* (London 1962); A. Benoit *Baptème, Sacrement d'Unité* (Paris 1971) pp. 11-84; G. Kretschmar 'Die Geschichte der Taufgottesdienstes in der alten Kirche' in *Leturgia* V (Kassel 1970) pp. 1-348.
2. See, for example, C. H. Ratschow *Die eine christliche Taufe* (Gütersloh 1972).
3. See, for example, J. Amougou-Atangana *Ein Sakrament des Geistesempfang? Zum Verhältnis von Taufe und Firmung* (Freiburg 1974).
4. Cf. Kretschmar *Leturgia* V pp. 291-3.
5. See the various reports brought out about the various meetings called to examine mutual recognition of each other's baptism.
6. *Ordo Baptismi Parvulorum* (Typ. Polygl. Vaticanis 1969). The *Ordo Initiationis Christianae Adultorum* was published in 1972.
7. The *Ordo Confirmationis* appeared in 1971.
8. I am relying mainly on the Gelasianum Vetus (ed. Mohlberg *Liber Sacramentorum Romanae Aeclesiae Ordinis Anni Circuli* (Rome 1960) pp. 42-54

and 67-74, and Ordo Romanus 11 (ed. Andrieu *Les Ordines Romani du Haut Moyen-Âge* vol. II (Louvain 1948) pp. 380 ff.

9. H. M. Riley *Christian Initiation* (Washington 1974).

10. Kretschmar *Leiturgia* V p. 238 (bibliography).

11. H. J. Auf der Maur *Die Osterhomilien des Asterios Sophistes* (Trier 1967).

12. F. X. Funk *Didascalia et Constitutiones Apostolorum* (Paderborn 1905).

13. G. Kretschmar 'Nouvelles recherches sur l'initiation chrétienne' in *La Maison-Dieu*, 132 (1977) pp. 7-32, esp. p. 18.

14. E. Yarnold, 'Baptism and the pagan mysteries in the fourth century', in *Heythrop Journal* 13 (1972) pp. 247-267.

15. B. Botte (ed.) *La Tradition Apostolique de Saint Hipployte* (Münster 1963) pp. 32-59.

16. F. Gistelinck, 'Doopbad en Geestesgave bij Tertullianus en Cyprianus' in *Ephemerides Theologicae Lovanienses* 43 (1967) pp. 532-556.

17. See, for example, *Didascalia* (ed.) Funk pp. 20-211.

18. G. W. Lampe *The Seal of the Spirit* 2nd ed. (London 1967).

19. Cf. Kretschmar *op. cit.* pp. 27-32.

20. B. Neunheuser 'Erwägungen zur ältesten Taufliturgie' in *Kyriakon*, Festschr. J. Quasten II (1970) pp. 709-723; A. Benoit *Baptême, Sacrement d'Unité* (Paris 1971) pp. 13-27.

21. S. Legasse'Baptême juif des prosélytes et baptême chrétien' in *Bull. de litt. ecclésiastique* 77 (1976) pp.3-40.

22. E. Stommel'Christliche Taufriten und antike Badesitten' in *Jahrbuch für Antike u. Christentum* 2 (1959) pp. 5-14.

23. Th. Klauser 'Taufet in lebendigem Wasser (*Did.* 7, 1-3)', *Gesammelte Arbeiten zur Liturgiegeschichte . . ., Jahrbuch für Antike und Christentum* 3 (1974) pp. 177-83; J. Daniélou 'Le symbolisme de l'eau vive' in *Rev. des Sciences Réligieuses* 32 (1958) pp. 335-346; W. Rordorf'Le baptême selon la Didachè' in *Mélanges Liturgiques Dom Botte* (Louvain 1972) pp. 499-509.

24. G. G. Willis 'What was the earliest Syrian baptismal tradition?' in *Studia Evangelica VI, Texte u. Untersuchungen* 112 (1973) pp. 651-654.

25. R. Pesch 'Zur Initiation im Neuen Testament' in *Liturgisches* Jahrbuch 21 (1971) pp. 90-107; G. Lohfink 'Der Ursprung der christliche Taufe' in *Theologisches Quartalschrift* 156 (1976) pp. 35-54; G. Haufe'Taufe und Heiliger Geist im Urchristentum' in *Theologische Literaturzeitung* 10 (1976) pp. 562-566.

Adrien Nocent

Christian Initiation and Community

SOME readers will doubt that this topic can still elicit any thoughts worth setting down. In order to avoid a profusion of commonplace judgments one is tempted to concentrate on the anthropological aspects of the question. A wholly or even largely anthropological treatment of the theme would, however, remove any real hope that the human sciences could be of help to liturgical theology. The too direct confrontation of anthropology with liturgical practice does no more than take us back to tedious experiments and to those approximations which result from the parallel use of inadequately refined methodologies. One calls to mind in this regard the examples of comparative liturgy and comparative religion, and the examination of the structure and theology of sacrifice in order to produce a type of concept which, when applied to Christ's sacrifice, proved constrictive and reductive, and eventually wrongheaded. If they are to be used to study liturgical practice, the human sciences have to devise appropriate instruments and adapt them, under pain of a certain degree of Nestorianism, to the rule of the divine incarnation characteristic of that liturgy of which Christ himself is the first celebrant. Hence I prefer to start from the liturgical experience itself, today as in the past, and in Scripture, while at the same time welcoming the assistance of anthropologists.

COMMUNITY AND INITIATION IN THE NEW TESTAMENT

In the New Testament itself we are given an account of the experience of Christian initiation and the community. The word *ekklesia* is met with in three closely linked aspects: the Christian assembly at worship, the local community in all its dimensions, and the universal Church—of which the local church is no mere part but, on the contrary, the total presence. This is not a new finding. One need only consult the article on the word *ekklesia* by K.L. Schmidt in the *Theologisches Wörterbuch* (1937) to discover what Vatican II was to draw out more explicitly. While stressing the importance of the diocese as the local church, with the bishop as its head and centre,[1] Schmidt also sees in the priest delegated by the bishop the presence of the bishop himself in the various legitimate assemblies of the faithful.[2]

The initiate comes into contact with the assembly in the act of celebration. But even before encountering it during his catechumenate, in the act of baptism and during the mystagogy, he has been in touch with one or another member of the local church who has introduced him to their experience of life. On coming into contact with the local community the initiate acquires his citizenship in the universal Church. There is, however, no question of a communitarian ghetto (a danger not always escaped by present-day attempts at catechumenal renewal). And we do not have to discern in this local community a sociological structure akin to that of purely human societies. Here the visible structure is an intimately meaningful sign of an invisible reality. Hence there is no reason to see a sociological structure on the one hand, and the Body of Christ (at a higher level) on the other hand. The initiate is not introduced to the presence of a visible sociological structure which then allows him access to the divine reality of the Body of Christ and the Trinity as presented in the New Testament.[3] The local community which welcomes the candidate to initiation is not enmeshed in a juridical structure; it is 'one' in the sense required by Christ in John 17, and the eucharistic celebration continually vitalises this ecclesial entity.

THE FATHERS OF THE CHURCH

The Fathers do not always accord with Paul on the 'ecclesial Body'. Under the influence of the nascent canonical system towards the end of the third century, the Fathers conceived of the Church as a sociologico-juridical structure, and the *sphragis* to which they often refer is for them primarily a sign of belonging to the body led by the same head towards the same goal. Though this perspective is not incorrect, it does not wholly accord with the notion of the 'one' in John, nor with the concorporeality which Cyril of Jerusalem discerned among the initiates. The reality of such a community into which the initiate was integrated is not properly accessible to anthropology; it demands the forging of a research method that will evoke this specific reality. What is in question is a community whose every member is born from above and is concorporeal with the others. These two aspects are emphasised more or less strongly by the New Testament in accordance with the catechetical needs of the local church. Peter, in a quasi-hymnal literary form, stresses the new state of the initiate who is intimately joined to the community.[4] John (in the gospel of John at least) emphasises the sacramental sign of water which, with the Spirit, allows the initiate his birth from above.[5]

CONTEMPORARY RITUALS

As far as our present-day rituals are concerned, there is a clear distinction between infant and adult baptism—a separation quite unknown in early Christianity. In the present-day initiation of adults, the rite is most authentic and in itself best expresses the relation between initiate and community. There is a real process from naming to taking part in the eucharist. Recovery of the progressive stages of the examination and the 'traditions' (handings over) of the Gospel, the Credo, the Pater and the responsible presence of the community shows clearly how an important event changes the life of the local church. The community of the convoked has become a divine convocation and the same community constitutes itself as the minister of that which it has received. It is this that Paul expresses when he says that the community is a minister of reconciliation.[6] This is conveyed in baptism and in confirmation, but supremely in the eucharist. It is not therefore a piece of futile pseudo-archaeology to restore the sacramental unity of the three stages of initiation. Hence the community enacts its relation to the initiate who advances towards it during Lent; this is not only an individual ascesis, but the concern of the entire community in prayer, fasting and charity for those who are to be initiated. There is therefore a dual movement that becomes very clear in the new adult ritual: that of the candidate to baptism and that of the community. This desire to meet is shown at several points in the ritual—I have noted at least thirty. Compared with the primitive rituals, our own tends in the catechumenal liturgy to multiply the tangible signs of interaction between initiate and community. In the baptismal ritual itself and in the confirmation rite there is an obvious intention to encourage greater participation by the community, for example in the two new formulas for the blessing of the water, which nevertheless deserve the criticism that they dispense with the typology that is so necessary for understanding the sacrament.

DEFECTS OF THE RITUAL

I should like to stress three points which I think do not fit the desire to signify the encounter between initiate and community. The first is the retention of the imperative baptismal formula, *Ego te baptizo*—the triple interrogation is administered *before* the sacramental baptismal rite. Though this introduction of the imperative formula is understandable in the case of infants who cannot respond to the celebrant's questioning, it seems unacceptable for an adult, the more so because it impairs in this case the dialogue between the celebrant (the Lord's representative) and the initiate who, in our ritual, has no visible part to play in the sacramental act of his own initiation. The offer of the gift of faith is made by the Lord through the minister who also represents the community. It is awe-inspiring to hear the initiate utter the acceptance of this gift of faith in the very action of his immersion in death with Christ, in order to be reborn together with him into a new life, by proclaiming the faith by which he is saved. To be sure the new ritual presents the rite of immersion as a possibility but does not offer any justification for it, and furthermore does not present it as the most significant part. One must remember, however, that the old texts represented not only the baptistery as *taphos,* a tomb, but also as the bosom of the Church, and as *mèter,* the mother who gives birth. There is also the inscription which Sixtus V had graven on the Lateran baptistery and in which he declared that there the Church as mother gave birth to its children of all races. In addition to the obvious meaning which immersion and emergence from the water have (that is, new birth and not only an effacement of sin through ablution), this rite primarily signifies the maternal intervention of the whole Church which, together with the Spirit, allows birth into the new life and into the faith.

Quite apart from the major defects of the new rite of confirmation, one may legitimately ask why the anointing formula has not been adopted from the Gelasian sacramentary—not because it is venerable but because it expresses meaningfully the entry of the baptized into the divine family. While signing the confirmand's forehead after the laying on of his hand, the bishop said: 'Signum Christi!'[7] The Spirit gives the confirmed person the countenance of Christ, so that the Father acknowledges in this Christian his own Son; he is taken into the community of the divine Persons which is an essential feature of the Christian community. The new confirmation rite nevertheless stresses ten times or so the activity of the community.

The 'language' of the adult rite deserves examination in regard to the expression of community. Here, however, I have restricted my comments to the most salient points.

The infant initiation rite is often described as successful. That is true, if one were to consider it only in terms of present-day theological and pastoral feeling. That would be satisfactory as long as important aspects were not obscured as a result, which would seem to be the case. Here again I shall restrict myself to only a few remarks in this respect. The points in question seem important though I realise that what I say could evoke criticism or indifference.

The infant baptism rite includes an excellent introduction which emphasises the intimate link between the three sacraments of initiation. They are not only mentioned but their usual order is respected: baptism, confirmation, eucharist. Attention is also given to the catechesis of the parents and those with responsibility for the child that is to be initiated.

I shall begin with this last point. The rite provides for this catechesis outside any liturgical and community perspective. The catechesis is not primarily *intra ipsa mysteria* and one in which the whole community takes a part. Here the activity of the local community in its various aspects has been overlooked. It is well to remember how the seventh-century Church (and the Church at an even later date) conceived of this catechesis. Of course it was not performed exclusively within a liturgical celebration, but the latter was acknowledged to be indispensable. The Gelasian sacramentary retains the practice of the three dominical examinations during Lent, though most of the time infant baptism is in question, for the catechesis of parents and godparents is in mind.[8] Roman Ordo nine transferred these examinations to weekdays but doubled their number. The weekday celebration already meant a reduction in the importance of the examinations, yet the increase in number betokens a desire to increase the emphasis on the liturgical catechesis of those responsible for the child. Though the entire community did not participate, as was the case with the three Sundays in Lent, the six quadragesimal meetings do show a concern on the part of the entire local church responsible for the catechesis of parents and godparents.[9] The Gelasians of the eighth century continued this practice. At Liège in September 1718, Edmond Martène saw the manuscript containing the examinations which were still celebrated at Liège, as they were at Vienne, Dauphiné.[10] Cardinal Sanctori, who died in 1602, had suggested in his ritual (which was not accepted by Paul V) that these examinations should be carried out.

Admittedly, one may ask whether these celebrations were not a matter of ceremony rather than retained with an explicit intention of making the entire community take part in a liturgical catechesis. In fact, there was a gradual diminution of the significance of the community aspect of initiation. Ordo nine and the weektime examinations are evidence of that. The theology of the twelfth century and its rather individualistic approach to the sacrament, and the infant mortality rate of the time, led to decisions resulting in the decree *Quam primum* which was taken up in canon law.[11] Circumstances have now changed and the Church approves of the baptism of groups of infants in the midst of the community. But there is a serious lack of the community's support in communal celebrations stressing the major aspects of parental catechesis. A creative task remains to be performed here and is requisite both for the rites and for the euchology.

As for the initiation rites themselves, without wishing to revive pastoral disagreements, there is no situation which lays less emphasis on the encounter of the initiate with the community. I do not assert that we have to restore a former, obsolete situation, but we should at least be aware that its abandonment has had results that have to be set against the pastoral advantages of present-day practice. Three facts should be noted: the space of time between the celebration of the three stages of infant initiation, the reversal of the eucharist and confirmation and, primarily in regard to the eucharist, the reduced significance of entry into the local church in infant baptism.

It is incorrect to say that the Eastern practice of administering the three sacraments of initiation to infants was followed only for a short time in the Western Church. A manuscript from eleventh-century Rome bears the rubric, *Si episcopus adest, statim confirmari opportet, postea communicari corpore et sanguine domini.* [12] But several—for example, French—manuscripts from the fifteenth century still bear the same rubric. However the rubric sometimes reads, *si eipscopus non adest, a presbytero communicetur infans.* There was at least a desire not to separate the eucharist from the initiation given in baptism. Furthermore, some Roman rituals include, after baptism, an invocation to the Father for the gifts of the Spirit as a kind of substitute for confirmation; then the eucharist was administered to the child. [13] Today infant baptism may be celebrated during the eucharist, though this does no more than emphasise a degree of artificiality in the procedure, for the baby does not take communion. I shall not stress the contradiction between the *praenotanda* of the infant baptism rite and its proper sense of the unity of the three sacraments of initiation; I merely emphasise the fact that the latter is not expressed in terms of unity of time, and that confirmation and the eucharist are reversed.

In regard to the eucharist, one must admit that it signifies and actualises at its highest point the entry of the initiate into the community. But a particular contemporary notion of pastoral practice would see the sacraments of confirmation and the eucharist differently, demanding an awareness for their reception which it does not demand in the case of baptism, which nevertheless comprises the first decisive step in conversion and entry into the Church.

However, the new ritual has given considerable attention to the major link between infant baptism and the faith of the ecclesial community. There are frequent references to the responsibility of the community and almost too many to that of the parents. There is a somewhat artificial declaration to the baby of the joy of the community into which it is welcomed. The community does indeed welcome the infant, but not to its table; and of course the baby does not understand what is said to it on the community's behalf.

CONCLUSIONS

Without continuing my analysis of the rite as it deserves, for instance from the linguistic viewpoint, I shall give my conclusions. In spite of several interventions of the community provided for by the ritual, it is still possible for its activity to be extremely formal. After the initial indispensable constitution of a true community, there would seem to be an urgent need to prepare a rite of catechesis for the parents and those responsible for the child; this should of course be a rite in which the community plays its part. In several instances, this infant catechumenate could resolve the serious problem of parents who are inadequately Christian yet request baptism for their child. In such cases a mode of catechumenate could provide a useful waiting-period easily acceptable to all concerned.[14]

Though I should like much greater latitude for creative endeavour in the adaptation of the euchology and even some rites, I should just like to say again that the barrier to any search for an authentic ritual is not theological but 'theologistic': the candidate is required to know everything possible about the confirmation and eucharist he is to receive, yet he does not have to be aware of the baptism that he receives. But we cannot change an attitude with which the Western Church has been impregnated for a good five centuries and which has led it to adopt a pastoral practice that is generally accepted. The present ritual we have been given is acceptable as a whole; but we can improve it in order to bring out more the link between initiation and the community.

Translated by John Griffiths

Notes

1. *Christus Dominus,* II, 1.
2. *Lumen Gentium,* 26, 1.
3. Eph. 2:19; 1 Tim. 3:15.
4. 1 P. 1:3; 2:25; 3:18-22.
5. Jn. 17:11; 20-6.
6. 2 Cor. 5:8.
7. L. C. Mohlberg *Liber Sacramentorum Romanae Aeclesiae Ordinis Anni Circuli.* Rerum Ecclesiasticarum documenta (series maior; Fontes IV) (Rome 1968) n. 452.
8. *Ibid.* nn. 283-328.
9. M. Andrieu *Les Ordines Romani du Haut Moyen-Âge.* Spicilegium sacrum lovaniense (1960) vol. 2, pp. 417-47.
10. E. Martène *De Antiquis Ecclesiae Ritibus,* lib. I, c. 1; A.-G. Martimort *La Documentation Liturgique de Dom Edmond Martène* Studi e Testi (Vatican City 1978) 279, p. 260, n. 391.
11. *Codex Iuris Canonici,* can. 770; cf. *La Maison-Dieu* 32 (1952) pp. 118-28.
12. Bibl. Vaticane, Barberini 564, fol. 67.
13. Bibl. Vallicelliana C. 32, fol. 36 r.
14. See the suggestions in this respect in *La Maison-Dieu* 104 (1970) pp. 41-64; *Notitiae* 61 (February 1971) pp. 64-73.

Willem Berger and Jan Van Der Lans

Stages of Human and Religious Growth

INTRODUCTION

THE ORIGINAL title given us by the editor of this issue of *Concilium* was: Stages and Duration Necessary to the Maturation of the Human Act and the Act of Faith. Now we are both psychologists but we have also both completed our theological training in preparation for the priesthood. As it stood, therefore, the heading reminded us of the distinction, often used in textbooks of moral theology, between an action seen as simply performed by a human being (*actus hominis*) and an action seen as consciously understood and intended (*actus humanus,* the fully human act). The 'human act' therefore entailed such aspects as control, liability and above all responsibility, and for that reason was taken as showing a person's ability to think and decide for himself.

This distinction opened the door to some wisdom and compassionate understanding when judging people's behaviour. It was based on a view, embodied in, for instance, Dutch criminal law, that there are people who cannot really see why what they did was wrong or, when they see it, are incapable of behaving accordingly. And so the law gives the judge the opportunity to decide whether a delinquent should be punished at all or, at most, should only be given a reduced sentence. Such a person, however, must be 'treated', meaning: helped to be cured of his 'mental illness'. This mental illness or disturbance occurs rather frequently and is then seen to spring from a disturbance experienced in the process of growing up.

Now it is obviously not our intention to deal here with problems of the administration of the law or of the application of penal law. We only bring it up in order to remind all of us of the fact that the distinctions which make us talk about the maturity or immaturity of people's behaviour spring from what we know to be true in our own experience. It is nevertheless clear that all the major religions interpret this universal urge present in all of us to become 'fully human' as a personal calling and that, particularly in Christianity, it is understood as a personal response to what is experienced as a personal call addressed to each of us. In so far as our study is concerned, the question may be formulated this way: What do we really know about how children become responsive to persuasion, and how in this process of persuasion and response can we recognise a development of freedom and particularly of growth in the way in which children hear and respond to the voice of God?

We may, of course, do better to put the last part of the question more modestly, in the form: What do we know about the way in which religious stimuli are received and responded to? The answers to this question are not exactly overwhelming, in fact, they are rather disappointing. We can only hope that our report on this matter will encourage more research and experiment. This is all the more important since it is now clear that the process of transmitting the faith, of 'tradition' in the original sense of the word, is today stagnating in many places and for many reasons.

THE PHASES OF A CHILD'S DEVELOPMENT

Psychological research seems at present to be very keen on researching the various stages through which a child passes in the process of growing up. Literature on this topic continues to increase in volume and quality. For his study of what chances a person has of developing religiously the Swedish psychologist of religion, Hjalmar Sundén, started by referring to P. Oesterrieth's survey of developmental psychology at large. And although this survey has been and still is being improved upon, it is good enough to serve our present purpose.

During the first four weeks the child's vegetative functions settle down. From the fifth week on the child begins to explore its surroundings. This goes on for some six months mainly by looking and listening, and later by touching and grasping. Thus the child begins to develop a number of sensori-motor patterns which will prove of fundamental importance for all later experiences. During the same period it begins to grow socially through some kind of relationship: the mother is recognised and even granted a smile; her gestures and expressions as well as those of other already familiar persons are apparently understood in some way.

From the ninth month to the fifteenth the child begins to handle objects in some sort of sequence and to experiment with combinations. It seems to react to the feelings of others, to the 'outside' and wants to entertain these people. It becomes shy in the presence of strangers and in new situations. It watches what adults are doing and begins to imitate them.

A recent study by Marian Riksen-Walraven has beautifully shown how much this development of explorative behaviour is influenced by the attention paid by the mother and the scope of her contact. Differences here revealed significant and corresponding differences in the explorative behaviour of the children.

Between the fifteenth and thirtieth months, when the child is two-and-a-half, it begins to stand up, to walk and even tries to speak. In all this it begins to show a certain independence of behaviour. It is quite capable of saying 'no' in a forceful way, can resist and even occasionally tyrannise its immediate surroundings. It intrudes into everything but at the same time lives in a world which is exclusively its own. From this world it keeps on watching and then imitates. By the end of the second year it begins to think.

Between the ages of 2½ and 6 the child begins to get interested in its peers but is not at all certain about how to relate to them. According to Gesell what is striking at this age is the way in which the child combines a kind of conformism with a determination to be itself. It begins to be more flexible in its movements and more certain of itself. Through verbal communication it begins to perceive the world as being structured. It begins to struggle out of the 'here and now', to imagine situations and to experiment with situations of the 'as if' kind. Curiosity increases and with it the attempt to try out 'daring' behaviour. It begins to show some sense of cooperation. During this phase, particularly between the ages of 3 and 3½ its tendency to anthropomorphise reaches its climax. Finally, it seems that occasionally it is already capable of delaying gratification. Between the ages of 5½ to 6 and 9 the child begins to be aware of a new and bigger world, along with and distinct from that of the family. After 7 there is a period of tranquillity during which the child becomes more self-centred. But when it reaches the age of 8 it wanders into a new and wider field of experience. It becomes active, energetic and looks as if it is all the time trying to reach beyond itself. It turns its thoughts to the actual world and in them reveals a trend towards animism and magic. At the same time it learns to distinguish more clearly between its own private world and the world to which all the others belong. In fact it seems to live in three worlds: 1. a world of its own, secret and full of fantasy and fairy-tales, where anything goes; 2. a world where everything is 'playing games', and 3. the real world of everybody. About the age of 8 it begins to hunger for more knowledge about this peculiar world which belongs to everybody, and such topics as geography and history stimulate it immensely.

It looks as if between the ages of 9 and 13 this development reaches a kind of completion: things and people begin to interest the youngster more than himself. On the other hand, one can clearly observe a growth in self-determination and self-criticism. This self-control seems to develop on the lines of 'knowing what you want'. About the age of 10 one notices a remarkable balance, a willingness to adapt; there is calm and trust. Some researchers even talk of the 'perfect age of the child'. Others point out that these 'teenagers' show a growing fear of the future and of being a failure. The youngster begins to understand something about judging others and himself. At this stage the meaning of 'ought to' in order to 'behave correctly' is accepted, and it has grown through contact with adults. From this stage on, it is the peers who decide the 'ought to' but the youngster realises that it has a say in the matter and a contribution to make to whatever is decided.

Between the ages of 11 and 13 intellectual abilities develop in a way that is both accelerated and decisive. When it reaches the age of 13 the typically extrovert trend in the child's development switches over to its opposite, and it turns inward and becomes more introvert.

RELIGIOUS AWARENESS IN CHILDHOOD

At the age of about 4-5 the child begins to ask questions: Where does everything come from? Who made it all? It wants to know who made the world, where does man come from, and what is 'dying'? Adults react to the child's curiosity in many different ways. One of the answers to these questions, given in a spirit of embarrassment or conviction, usually refers to God or Jesus. Whatever the case may be, religion inserts itself into the life of the child through its social surroundings. This means that the approach of the child to religion is determined by the way it is influenced by the parents. When—as is often the case—the child begins to develop an attitude of trust in God, it reflects its attitude to its father. And so the provisional and concrete ways in which the child thinks about God show the ways in which it thinks of its father.

For the rest, we know very little indeed about the religious life of small children. A child usually slips into the religious milieu in which it finds itself, without great difficulties. It is so open to suggestion that it adopts ways of thinking and behaving which are in no way representative of personal experience. Since the child, at this stage, wants to see things as much as possible in concrete images, the telling of stories from the bible is, from the educational point of view, much more valuable than explanation and catechism.

In this way the small child develops an image of God which in all probability meets its strong need to understand and to explore. But it is not enough when the child feels in need of help or is in distress. The child understands, however, that this God is somebody to whom the parents turn with reverence, in silence, and in all kinds of impressive ways.

According to Börjeson and Larson it may occasionally happen that a child of 9 or 10 shows for the first time some true religious feeling of its own. This has been sometimes confirmed by students who told us about their own religious development. The same Börjeson and Larson suggest on the basis of all this: 1. that conscious 'religion' does not occur before the ages of 9-10; and 2. that before this age separate religious instruction (the authors have the 'Sunday school' in mind) serves no purpose whatever: the children inevitably twist everything they are told. The same conclusions were reached by Gordon Allport, Rümke and the religious educationist Lee. On the other hand, Vergote agrees with Thun and Klingberg who maintain that 'the child is a religious being in its own way' and 'thinks' God in terms of an open and naïve anthropomorphism. Klingberg holds that religious experience can already occur in early childhood and religious life can reach remarkable depth in the later stages of this childhood. Klingberg's findings are supported by those of Ulrieke Hörberg in her study, *Barn och Religion* (The Child and Religion).

CAN ONE SPEAK OF STAGES OF RELIGIOUS DEVELOPMENT?

The title of this article includes the term 'growth'. Now growth is a term of biological origin. The biological factors involved in a child's development make it possible to distinguish stages according to a common norm. But this development is at the same time very much influenced by learning and experience. Experience arises when the child takes over patterns of observation and behaviour from its social environment. Such observation and patterns of behaviour obviously differ considerably from one culture to another and even between one individual and another. In one a-religious family grandparents play a part and transmit some religious traditions while this is wholly lacking in some other a-religious family. And it is not merely a matter of people either: there may be vast differences in the material or geographical conditions. The view of a cemetery may make one think of death, while sayings about Christ, the one who overcame death and the grave, can then assume a meaning of which other children are totally ignorant (Andrae, 1933).

This implies a certain criticism of empirical studies which too easily give the impression that religious development depends more on age than on environment. In the past, research in the field of a child's religious development relied more on the evidence of literature and autobiography which clearly brought out more clearly the influnce of the environment. The way growing and learning are related, particularly in the area of religion, is basically determined by the influence of the parents, and especially the mother. This is why we want to look carefully at the stages of development as described by W. Gruehn.

1. Gruehn maintains that he observed the first attempt at prayer at the age of 1½.

2. Between 2 and 4 he speaks about a pre-magic stage. When the environment is favourable the child begins really to pray and to have some idea about God. But at the same time its religiousness is rather 'wild and unrestrained': God, the child Jesus, angels and witches belong to the same world.

3. The 'magic stage' lasts from 4-7: the child sees God mainly as a kind of magician and prays to Him to do anything he wants, even what is wrong.

4. From 7 on the worry about 'naughty and nice', 'good and bad', 'fair and unfair' (or 'good and bad') prevails. The idea of God is anthropomorphic: God is a kind of man of supernatural proportions.

Gruehn's scheme assumes a pre-religious stage. The transition from this stage to the first religious stage is important, and Gruehn sees the mother as the person who presides over this process. In this he relies on the research undertaken by Vogel. Many researchers consider this pre-religious stage significant, since this stage sees the development of all the functions which make a religious life possible. Here the differentiation between child and mother is particularly important because the formation of an interpersonal relationship is the direct preparation for religious experience.

During this period the child begins to realise that it exists in its own right, distinct from the rest of the world. And then the relationship with the mother becomes the prototype of all other relations. Some psychologists of religion, like D. H. Salman, feel that the image of the mother may constitute in the child's mind the first draft of his idea about God: an omniscient, perfect, loving person on whom everything depends and whose love produces the gift of life. This obviously does not yet come over in a conceptual way, but it is an experience which expresses itself through affectionate or other behaviour towards a partner. In a practical sense the child is aware of the reality of this partner and at the same time learns to behave in a way which fits in with this relationship. Paul Vogel maintained that a child with a religious mother who prays shows signs of a religious life before it can even talk. He called this first stage the 'period of wordless mother-religion'. For Vogel the second stage occurs when the child learns to talk, gets some *idea* of an object and begins to act consciously. It is possible that, to start with, the child has God and its mother all mixed up but gradually begins to sort them out when it begins to talk and to say its first prayers. Vogel describes this stage as that of *betende Mutterreligion* (prayerful mother-religion) and suggests that it may last up to the age of 8.

If we agree with Gruehn that we have a pre-magic stage between 2 and

4, then the significance of the praying mother (or, in today's families, the praying parents) is hardly important. It is probable that the child knows quite well when his parents are telling him a story and when they are praying with him. If this is true, the child can also see the difference between God and the characters that figure in fairy-tales. This makes it difficult to attribute much validity to Gruehn's 'wild religious imaginings of the child'. These imaginings must be seen in connection with the factors that prevail in the child's environment.

Sundén would prefer to describe this stage as 'the age of religious discoveries'. He stresses the importance of the fact that the child is perfectly free to explore quite spontaneously the piety of the adults and what God means in their lives. Salman offers four ways of judging whether a child has made such discoveries: the spontaneous refusal to budge, the willingness to listen, quiet attention, and quiet joy.

It appears indeed that at this stage the child can develop an emotional inclination to pray. It distinguishes between the kind of silence that goes with illness or sleep and the silence that is required for prayer.

Gruehn thinks that between the ages of 4 and 7 children see God as a kind of magician. Sundén would prefer to qualify this by saying that at this age children can be very insistent about God's power. Klingberg's research shows how much children can rely on this power. There are two points in the matter discussed so far which need mentioning. First of all, Bovet has pointed out that at the age of 6 children begin to realise that their parents cannot know everything. In the right circumstances this may make a child's religious life more intense and strengthen his trust in God. According to Vergote such circumstances assume a religious atmosphere in the family and religious practice. These factors make the child realise that parents are subject to God.

During this stage children may also go through a further important experience: they find out about the inevitability of death. This discovery may well make the child more religious. But when the child identifies God with death ('Mummy is with God'), it may well expel both, and then there is an end to prayer and anything to do with religion.

The landmarks which Gruehn discerned during the period from 7-15 have also been subjected to scrutiny. For Gruehn the main feature of this period was the anthropomorphic image of God. But in 1962 Clavier found this an oversimplification of the facts. He found that at the age of 6 and 7 this anthropomorphism was simple and materialistic; at the age of 8 or 9 God is just human but with a margin: He and His throne are surrounded by angels, and you neither may nor can touch Him. When the child reaches the age of 12 the idea of God has become more spiritual: God is everywhere and invisible.

IS IT 'GROWING' OR 'LEARNING'?

Have we now any better idea of what in religious development should be attributed to learning and what to growing?

In 1967 Decouchy tried to decide the issue by concentrating on the anthropomorphic image of God. He did so by trying to pin down what children who had been subjected to Catholic catechetics associated the word 'God' with, and observed this at various ages. He found that from 9-10 God is seen as great, omniscient, omnipresent, good and just. Round about the age of 12 and 13 God is seen as Lord, Redeemer, Father. 15-year olds are inclined to look rather at the more inward aspects of the problem: they are concerned with love, prayer, obedience, a comforting dialogue, as well as doubts and fear.

Sundén nevertheless questions whether the researcher has got hold here of results that are due to growth or to instruction, the more so since catechetical instruction introduces various ages to different images and attributes of God. Yet, Decouchy thinks it highly probable that we have to do here with the way the influences of age and growth affect the issue.

As mentioned above, Gruehn based his scheme of the stages of religious growth mainly on the child's changing image of God. Goldman took a different line, closely following Piaget's theory of the development of intelligence. Since Piaget holds that this development has a biological foundation, none of the stages can be left out. These stages are:

1. sensori-motor intelligence, up to the age of 2;
2. the pre-operational stage, from 2-4;
3. the intuitive stage, from 4-7;
4. the concrete operational stage, from 8-11;
5. the formal operational stage, from 11-14.

Goldman maintains that as long as the child has not yet reached stage 4, it is still pre-religious, but at stage 4 he describes the child as sub-religious. At stage 5 the youngster is quite likely to take a negative line with regard to religion but this may well develop into a truly positive and personal attitude. Sundén does not agree that all children up to 8 should be labelled 'pre-religious', which seems to him far too narrow a view, particularly when one studies the material gathered by Klingberg.

THE GROWTH INTO ADULTHOOD AND RELIGION

In his study of 'the young Luther' E. K. Erikson wanted first of all to illustrate what he meant by 'identity crisis' and the process of discovering one's identity. He then wanted to show how, up to this crisis point, religious development must be interpreted and guided if it is to play a viable part in this process. Finally he discusses the funtion a guru or counsellor can and must fulfil in this situation. Although Sundén refers to Erikson's notion of 'identity crisis', he developed his own view of the way in which religious development can help to find one's own place in adult life. During childhood the 'I' develops first through identification with the mother, and then with other adults. But identification is not merely the projecting of an image. Identification with a parent means that a child can play two roles: it can talk *to* itself with the mother's voice and it can talk *as* itself to the mother as if she were present. The 'I' usually plays one role or another. Situations in which no role is played at all probably do not exist.

With puberty the role repertoire increases: the professional role, the sex role, and so on. These are new roles which must still be acquired and practised, and as long as this has not yet been achieved the youngster will feel very unsure of himself. Moreover, there may be conflicting roles, e.g., being a member of a gang and being son or daughter, or being a member of a religious community and being son, as happened in the case of Luther. Then a choice has to be made. The adolescent wonders who he really is, what he must become, what his vocation is or what is expected of him. The problem then is never simply: Who am I? but also : Have I got a partner, somebody I can lean on and to whom I myself can be loyal in the midst of all this role changing? If the adolescent has learned to pray and to live in a Christian environment, Christ may well come to fill this part.

Rümke has pointed out that, regardless of their environment, all adolescents begin to experience a sense of belonging in a meaningful way to the whole of reality, and that this whole reality is the origin and ground of their existence. Sometimes this experience of 'growing' is linked with words and images which are 'traditional' in their particular group. This may then lead to a relationship with this origin and ground which is felt as harmonious and continuing. On the other hand, the opposite may happen and the development of such a relationship will be profoundly disturbed.

CAN ANY CONCLUSIONS BE DRAWN FROM ALL THIS RESEARCH?

Vergote quotes the highly regarded H. Lubienski de Lenval as saying that she expects nothing from academic psychology. And H. Andriessen who, together with J. Habraken and P. Frijns, wrote a small book on the way faith springs from a child's experience, told us that, however carefully the religious development of children had been researched by psychologists, he was not satisfied with it for two reasons: it is difficult to embody the results in any scheme for introducing catechetics; but, above all, the results of this research would mainly show teaching devices, used in an educational system which is barely connected with the way in which children learn from their own experience. These authors want to try to make all those people who are keen on introducing children into a vast religious world, more genuinely anxious to look into the genuineness and value of their own religious convictions. Now, it seems to us that here we have at least an endeavour which does not conflict with what has been so generally observed. It is true that there is difference of opinion about the question at what stage one can speak of a child being 'religious'. But Sundén's criticism of Gruehn's way of arranging the stages makes it abundantly clear that the most important influence on a child's religious development is the relationship of the child with its parents. A separate and explicitly ecclesiastical introduction of the child to religion can never replace or improve upon the implicit way which happens naturally through the day-to-day relationship of the child with its parents. It seems sensible to encourage the parents to be and to show themselves as religious in this relationship.

Has all this anything to contribute to the 'initiation' or introduction of young adults to religion? From the psychological point of view the most important fact is in our view that genuine religious faith can only exist where it is rooted in personal experience and can find support in the way other people reveal their own religious experience. Today there are religious movements which are new and still hardly institutionalised and often show a faith which is strong, explicit and obviously influencing the whole of life. This sort of faith seems usually to have grown out of crisis situations such as the identity crisis which seem to have made those people receptive to a living faith and willing to share their own experience with others through their personal witness. Such mediation is indispensable. Here we see why in these movements the initiation ritual is more often than not the end and confirmation of a religious development rather than the beginning.

Translated by Theo Weston

Bibliography

Allport, G. *The Individual and his Religion* (New York 1951).

Andrae, T. *Det Osynligas Värld* (Stockholm 1933).

Andriessen, H., Habraken, J. & Frijns, F. *Als de boer wakker is. Het ontkiemen van geloof uit de ervaring van het kind.*

Börjeson, G. & Larsson, R. *Skolärens Psykologi* (Stockholm 1963).

Bovet, P. *Le Sentiment Réligieux et la Psychologie de l'Enfant* (Neuchâtel/Paris 1951).

Clavier, H. *L'idée de Dieu Chez l'Enfant* (Paris 1962).

Decouchy, J. P. *Structure Génétique de l'Idée de Dieu Chez les Catholiques Français* (Brussels 1967).

Gesell, A. *Child Development. An Introduction to the Study of Human Growth* (New York 1949).

Goldman, R. *Religious Thinking from Childhood to Adolescence* (London 1964).

Id. *Readiness for Religion* (London 1968).

Gruehn, W. *Die Frömmigkeit der Gegenwart* (Konstanz 1960).

Hörberg-Strake, V. *Barn och Religion* (Uppsala 1966).

Klingberg, G. *Grundskoleärens Psykologi* (Stockholm 1966).

Lee, R. S. *Your Growing Child and Religion* (New York 1963).

Oesterrieth, P. *Introduction à la Psychologie de l'Enfant* (Paris 1957).

Rikesen-Walraven, J. M. *Stimulering van de Vroeghinderlijke Ontwikkeling* (Amsterdam 1977).

Rümke, H. *Karakter en aanleg in Verband met het Ongeloof* (Amsterdam 1953).

Salman, D. H. 'Il primo sviluppo della personalità nel bambino christiano i Sacra Doctrina' *Revista Theologica d'Attualità dello Studio Domenicano di Bologna* 50 (1968) pp. 259-263.

Sundén, H. *Barn och Religion* (Karlskrona 1974).

Thun, Th. *Die Religion des Kindes* (Stuttgart 1959).

Vergote, A. *Godsdienstpsychologie* (The Hague 1967).

Vogel, P. 'Ein Beitrag zur Religionspsychologie des Kindes' *Archiv für die gesamte Psychologie* 96 (Liepzig 1936).

PART II

Bulletins

Luigi della Torre

Implementation of the *Ordo Initiationis Christianae Adultorum*: A Survey

SINCE 1972, the practical implementation of the *Ordo Initiationis Christianae Adultorum* (OICA—the *Order of Christian Initiation of Adults*)[1] has been entrusted to the local churches. Now, six years later (this article was written in the spring of 1978) what kind of assessment is it possible to make of the situation? Documentary research has yielded rather disappointing results, in the sense that articles published by the reviews contain almost exclusively theologico-liturgical explanations of the new rite or else directions (theoretical) for putting them into effect pastorally. For the present incomplete and at times generic survey, in addition to gleaning what facts I could from national publications, I had recourse to personal conversations with missionaries and missiologists whom I have had the opportunity to meet in Rome.

1. THE 'RECEPTION' OF OICA BY THE LOCAL CHURCHES

The OICA differs from the liturgical books hitherto published by Rome, because its implementation is not achieved simply through translation and ritual execution, as a substitute for other Latin books. It contains and proposes a new discipline for the preparation of candidates for baptism, which every local church is expected to consider carefully and adapt to its particular situation. It seems to me that the 'reception' each local church should accord this book is a typical example of the 'reception' it should accord *every* doctrinal or pastoral document, and every new liturgical rite issued by the Holy See. In the case of the liturgy, the act of acceptance not only 'verifies, recognises and attests that some-thing corresponds to the good of the Church'[2]; it takes place in the translation of the texts, in the local publication of the liturgical book, in the provision made by the bishop and national hierarchy for putting it into practice, in the various adaptations to indigenous culture envisaged by the book itself and is fully realised by the concrete implementation of the proposed ritual within the celebrating assembly.[3] This entire process of acceptance, which goes from the Latin liturgical book (the *editio typica*) to the actual celebration, has often taken place through literal trans-lations and ritual execution; but it would seem that the OICA does not tolerate such treatment, and that it challenges the local churches with a genuine task of discernment and adjustment. Something similar, moreover, was required in the case of the *Ordo Poenitentiae,* in that it was not intended as a substitute for an existing Latin ritual but was presented as introducing something new into Christian and ecclesial penitential practice. The relative lack of success of that *Ordo* compels one to reflect that the fate of the OICA has been no better. At least not yet.

(a) The translations

The first stage in the acceptance of a luturgical book is its translation from Latin into the local language. Just how delicate and complex an operation this is emerges clearly from ten years' practical experience, given that some countries are already feeling the need to review the translations they have adopted, the latter being judged to be unmean-ingful in terms of the local linguistic culture and impossible to com-municate in the assembly.[4] In the case of OICA I will restrict myself to listing the date of recognition (*confirmatio*) of the translations by the Congregation for Divine Worship, as reported in the periodical *Notitiae.* The name listed is that of the nation where the episcopate presented the translation for approval.

1973 Madagascar
1974 Ruanda, Brazil, Hungary (*Ordo Simplicior*), Yugoslavia (Croat translation), Vietnam, France and French-speaking areas, Zäire, USA and English-speaking areas.
1975 New Zealand (English translation).
1976 Korea, Spain, England and Ireland, Latin America (CELAM edi-tion in Spanish),[5] Chile, Paraguay, Uganda (Runyankolerukyga translation), Indonesia.
1977 Holland, southern Africa (Zulu translation), Honduras, Carib-bean, Peru.
1978 Japan, Italy.

Six years after the *editio typica,* the situation is not encouraging, though one should not be misled by this. In many parts of the world, and especially in the 'missionary' countries, use is being made of provisional and experimental translations, produced in many cases by priests, individually or in groups, and subsequently approved either by the local bishop or by the bishops' conference as a whole. These are translations, for the most part typewritten and Xeroxed, of the prayers and readings, while for the normative parts and the rubrics, recourse is had either to the Latin edition or to the European language editions. The general tendency, however, up until now, has been to translate the texts literally, without making any serious attempt to adapt them.

(b) Editions and episcopal instructions

In Germany the OICA was published in 1975 in a 'publication of the Liturgical Institutes of Zalburg, Trier and Zurich' as a 'study text' with an 'introduction' signed by four liturgists. The German translation was approved by the Congregation for Divine Worship in March 1971, prior, therefore, to the appearance of the *editio typica,* but not a word was said by the bishops regarding the liturgical use of this book. The English-language edition (US Catholic Conference, Washington DC, the text being 'provisional' but approved by Rome) and the Dutch edition (with the *imprimatur* of the Dutch episcopate) carried neither an 'introduction' nor a 'decree' from the local hierarchy or episcopal liturgical commission. The editions in Spanish, Portuguese and Italian were introduced by the bishops who, in most cases through the agency of their liturgical commission, assessed the significance and the importance of the OICA and made a number of suggestions for its use. Generally speaking one finds that in the countries of this linguistic area, where Christianity dates back to antiquity, the relevance of the book seems to be limited, since in almost every case baptism takes place shortly after birth. It is stated, however, as by the Spanish liturgical commission, that the OICA 'is not only concerned with the baptism of adults, but teaches us what Christian initiation requires both of the adult who asks for baptism and of the child . . . who, after adequate instruction (catechumenate) approaches the Eucharist for the first time, this completing his incorporation into the Body of Christ'. Furthermore, in the face of 'the widespread proliferation of movements which aim at recovering the catechumenal element in Christian formation', the OICA is presented as offering valid directives for the organisation and content of the catechumenate. The Italian Bishops' Conference recognises that 'the gradual and progressive itinerary from evangelisation to initiation, catechesis and mystagogy is presented in the OICA as the typical pattern for Christian formation'.

The most interesting edition is the French, because it comes across as functional even in its title: 'Ritual for the Baptism of Adults in Stages', and in the separate booklets of its typographical format. The introduction, signed by the national director for the catechumenate in France, is drawn up with doctrinal and pastoral assurance and practical purpose—evidence of the experience that has variously affected the French Church, which can afford to present an edition which is 'the adaptation for our own country of the Roman Missal'. There is nothing improvised about it: 'It was in the pipeline for years'—which means that it has been possible to put together a 'French ritual' in which even the contents of the normative part have been summarised, selected and restructured on the basis of proven pastoral *praxis*. The translation of the liturgical texts—the invitations (*nomitiones*) in particular, but also the prayers—has been carried through freely and creatively.

The French case seems to be unique, for even those editions from 'mission countries' which I have had the opportunity to examine contain a literal translation of the Latin texts and no evidence of adaptation to local culture. In their preface to the Lingala edition, the bishops of Zaïre state: 'Experiments will be carried out in the various regions of Zaïre. Later the Bishops' Conference will make additional changes and adaptations according to its competence.'

(c) Acceptance by pastoral workers and communities

Thanks to the initiatives of pastoral workers in parishes, catechetical centres and catechumenal groups, things are happening which the official editions have neither decreed nor encouraged. Experiments are taking place which will inevitably come to light and, if handled carefully, will be able to win official approval. But such information as I have been able to gather suggests that the area within which this experimentation is taking place is not very extensive and that there will be no significant short-term results. Why? Because priests are unprepared and the faithful indifferent. 'Many priests are unaware of its existence, or else have never laid hands on a copy', was the opinion of some 'itinerant catechists' from neo-catechumenal communities, whose travels have taken them all over Europe as well as throughout most of the Americas and a large part of Asia. In order to justify and explain their programme for a progressive itinerary of faith for baptised adults, they take the OICA as their point of reference and therefore have the opportunity to discuss it with the bishops and parish priests. It seems in fact that anyone who has had no need to make use of it either for practical purposes or for purposes of study does not consider he has a duty or a need to know anything about it. Even where the catechumenate has been officially established, the problem seems to relate to the priests and catechists involved in it; the other pastoral workers do not feel it concerns them. I was told by a missiologist, who, in 1977, visited Africa, where the OICA is studied in some catechetical institutes and catechetics is geared to the catechumenate, that seldom, either in programmes of study for catechists or among the concerns of the teachers, did he find any evidence of the guidelines set down in the OICA. Even those responsible for missionary activity admitted, when interviewed in Rome, that they found it difficult to provide information or make any kind of evaluation. Apart from one or two exceptional cases, we are still in the very early stages as far as pastoral awareness of the OICA is concerned.

The response of catechumens to renewed programmes of preparation for baptism has generally been favourable wherever the approach is serious and informed. They can compare the present guidelines with those of only a few years ago and they appreciate the longer time scale if it offers the possibility of a progressive assimilation of the Christian life that will guarantee fidelity. In Japan, converted pagans living in 'neo-catechumenal' communities have decided, in spite of the bishops' suggestion that they should receive baptism after two years, to put it off until the end of the period envisaged for growth in the faith.

With the exception of those small communities which draw inspiration for their journey of faith from the OICA and those parishes in which there is a substantial number of catechumens, the majority of the faithful are unaware of the fact that the Catholic Church has a new discipline for those who are seeking to become Christians.

One missionary, who worked from 1970 to 1977 in an African church which was in the vanguard of experimentation with the OICA even before the publication of the official text, declares that 'the Christian community is virtually unaware of the course followed by catechumens who are regarded only too easily as belonging to an inferior category'.

This same missionary explains the indifference of clergy and faithful as the result of their lack of any serious experience of conversion, either in terms of the practical integration of the Gospel into their daily lives or in terms of the sacramental celebration of newness of life, which means they are not open to the originality of the proposals contained in the OICA.

(d) The catechumenal perspective at the Synod of Bishops on catechesis

The publication of the OICA stimulated in the Catholic Church a process of reflection which led to a 'catechumenal' or what one might call an 'initiatory perspective' in catechetical and formative activity, not only in missionary countries, but also in churches which date back to the early ages of Christianity and which have to contend with such phenomena as the secularisation of the nominally Christian masses and the leakage of even educated children and young people from the various institutions of the Church.

This 'perspective', which made a tentative appearance at the 1974 Synod of Bishops, the theme of which was 'evangelisation in the modern world', was incorporated into the 'Message to all Christians' of the bishops who took part in the 1977 Synod: 'The profession of faith is, in catechesis, both the point of departure and the point of arrival. It is the purpose of catechesis to ensure that the community of believers proclaims that Jesus, the Christ, the Son of God, is alive and is the Saviour. For this reason the model of every form of catechesis is the baptismal catechumenate, the specific process of formation through which the adult convert to the faith is led finally to the profession of baptismal faith during the Easter Vigil. In the course of this preparation the catechumens receive the Gospel (that is the Sacred Scriptures) and its concrete ecclesial expression, which is the Creed.'[6]

Reading the interventions made during the plenary sessions and the summaries of the work of the *circuli minores,* one observes that this catechumenal perspective is common to bishops from the so-called 'missionary' countries and those from the so-called 'Christian' countries.[7] Although it is not explicitly stated, it is easy to deduce from the language used that these contributions to the work of the Synod derive from experience of the pre- or post-baptismal catechumenate, and from current catechetical research in the Church, both of which refer back directly or indirectly to the OICA. This growing climate of interest in the catechumenal forms of Christian initiation, of deepening awareness of their significance, together with a corresponding sense either of sterility produced by any kind of superficial implementation or of fruitfulness derived from initiatives carried through with fidelity and tenacity, constitutes the surest guarantee of a pastorally effective Christian initiation of adults in the future.

2. PARTICULAR PROBLEMS RELATED TO IMPLEMENTATION

Churches which were able to prepare themselves by means of experimentation prior to 1972—those of Rwanda-Burundi, for example, began as early as 1966—were certainly at an advantage when it came to the pastoral application of the OICA, and there is a notable difference between them and the others, which only began to consider the possibilities of a renewed catechumenal discipline when they received the *editio typica.* One gets the impression that the vanguard is moving ahead everywhere, and that an irreversible process has been started. On the other hand one is not surprised by local hesitation or by partial and

provisional achievements. It would seem that the OICA is being subjected everywhere to a process of interpretation and adaptation either by
the individual priests who use it or by groups of priests working together,
even if this is not apparent from the official documents.

(a) Catechumenate and courses of study

Attempts at adaptation have not always been intelligent or carried out
in the spirit of the OICA. Sometimes they amount to mere expedients for
adapting the proposals of the OICA or using its formularies in already
existing situations, with the net result that the latter are changed only in
appearance. This is what tends to happen particularly in missionary areas,
where preparation fo baptism takes place in conjunction with regular
courses of study, and the OICA gets used for a catechumenate, the 'adult'
members of which are children aged between 8 and 11 years. In one
edition of the OICA the following reason is given to justify the omission
from the translation of chapter V ('Rite for the Christian initiation of
children who are of an age to attend catechism classes'): 'Because, having
been integrated into the general pastoral programme of the parish, these
children are not accorded special rites for the liturgical stages of the
catechumenate and the rites of Christian initiation.' They therefore follow the celebratory itinerary which the OICA envisages for adults,
though with an inevitably childish experience of faith and conversion.
That the children in question are of primary school age is clear from an
observation in the same text: 'This only arises in one or two cases in the
secondary schools'.

This link between the path to the sacraments of Christian initiation and
a regular course of study raises serious problems on account of the
confusion it creates between initiation into the structures of civil life and
initiation into the life of faith. One gets the impression that the reasons for
seeking baptism and deciding to enter the Church are still determined by
socio-cultural factors, rather than in response to the divine call presented
as good news. In fact, one of the reasons most recently put forward, apart
from the belief that by joining a church one raises one's cultural and social
status, is marriage with a Catholic partner.

(b) The stages along the way

How is the division into stages envisaged in the OICA no. 6 (where
'times of searching and growth' are also envisaged) actually put into
practice? These stages are: the precatechumenate, the catechumenate,
the immediate and intense preparation (time of purification and illumi-
nation), and the post-baptismal stage of the mystagogy. In Rwanda-

Burundi, where the preparatory period lasts for four years, and in the French catechumenate, these different stages are respected, and the latter two usually coincide with Lent and the Easter season. In other places, however, the stages of the journey get adjusted to local conditions and established customs.

In certain regions of Uganda and Zaïre, for example, the 'times' correspond to the 'places' of catechesis, which are three in number: the village chapel (where the precatechumenate takes place), the principal church (where the first part of the catechumenate takes place under the guidance of a catechist), and the central church of the mission where the catechumens take up residence, working and preparing themselves for baptism, under the guidance of the missionary priest). This last stage takes between three and six months, and the series are arranged to alternate in such a way that only one terminates at Easter. In some places they run from September to Christmas (which becomes a baptismal feast) and from January to Easter.

Where there are only a few candidates, or even single individuals as in Japan, it is not possible to form a catechumenal group with its own activities; the preparation is carried out through meetings with the priest, the division into three periods, precatechumenate, catechumenate and preparatory phase, being respected, with a certain amount of ritual for the passage from one to the next—although the latter is not significant in the catechumens' experience of faith, perhaps because often enough the catechesis follows the conventional pattern, without any connection with concrete daily life or any reference to the signs celebrated.

(c) Celebration and symbolism

One of the concerns of the OICA is that the celebrations should genuinely correspond to the growth of experience and the process of conversion, and not simply be reduced to empty ritual—so much so that in no. 125 in connection with the 'tradition' or reading over of the *Credo* and the *Our Father,* which can be anticipated, it affirms that 'these celebrations must take place when the catechumens have reached a certain degree of maturity; otherwise they should be omitted'. From the experiences I have gathered together and examined, it seems that the complex ritual chosen by the pastors is the same everywhere and for all, given that attention is still concentrated on the things that need to be taught and celebrated, rather than on the people who are doing the learning and celebrating.

In the local editions of the OICA, in general no significant options emerge from among the various possibilities envisaged, and even less is there any record of attempts at adaptation contemplated or authorised by the bishops' conferences (nos. 64-65). One gets the impression that this is being done at the grass roots level by priests and catechists, who take initiatives that go beyond what is allowed by no. 67. There is probably no other practicable way of carrying out experiments which, when the opportune moment comes to examine them, may subsequently receive episcopal approval.

One often comes across the rite of the 'impositions of medals', a usage probably introduced by the missionaries. As far as I can make out, the absorption of elements of local culture in some places involves the incorporation of the local 'book of etiquette' into the rite of presentation to the community, or of certain oaths during the triple renunciation (in one place objects connected with superstition or divination are carried).

Reading the interventions of those bishops at the Synods of 1974 and 1977 who argued in favour of the indigenisation of the expression, including the symbolico-liturgical expression, of the faith of the Gospel, one is surprised to note that, where Christian initiation is concerned, almost nothing has been achieved in this direction. The explanation for this was given me by a missiologist familiar with both Africa and Asia: for these peoples faith is more closely associated with ritual practices than with doctrinal formulations, and Christian identity and ecclesial stability is seen in terms of liturgical customs, the true manifestations of orthodoxy. Conversion is expressed in concrete terms through the relinquishing of certain religio-ritual practices in favour of the liturgical practices of the Church; to find there the very elements one had left behind can be a source of anxiety, or even prove positively disorientating.

Translated by Sarah Fawcett

Notes

1. The *editio typica* of the OICA, of 6 January 1972, represents the realisation of the provisions of Vatican II, in the constitution *Sacrosanctum Concilium* on the liturgy nos. 64-71, and the decree *Ad Gentes* on the missionary activity of the Church, no. 14.

2. Y. Congar 'La réception comme realité ecclésiologique' *Concilium,* 7 (1972) p. 102.

3. Cf. A. Cuva 'La creatività rituale nei libri liturgici ai vari livelli di competenza' *Epheremides Liturgicae,* 89, 1975 pp. 54-99.

4. Cf. G. F. Venturi 'Fenomeni e problemi linguistici della tradizione liturgica nel passaggio da una cultura ad un'altra' *Ephemerides Liturgicae* 92, 1977 pp. 5-75.

5. The Spanish-language translation edited by CELAM was published in the

Ritual Conjunto de los Sacramentos (Bogota 1976); but each national church must ask Rome for permission to adopt it. This 'ritual', which gathers together in a single manageable volume all the sacramental rites, favours the diffusion of the OICA, but does not necessarily guarantee knowledge of it among pastors.

6. In *La Documentation Catholique* no. 21 (1977) p. 1018. It is likely that the 'catechumenal perspective' inspired the pontifical document, for the drafting of which the bishops voted on a number of propositions. A synthesis of the latter was published in *Osservatore Romano* (23 October 1978), p. 5. The first section of the final series is interesting: 'In the present situation, it is important to evaluate initiatives that are being taken to provide a catechumenate for those who are preparing for baptism and, in various areas where there is an authentic Christian tradition, to think of some form of catechesis which will enable the baptised to grow in awareness of their faith and help them to live in a consistent way. The introduction of a genuine catechumenate for the baptised is something that is being studied and tried out carefully.'

7. The interventions of the bishops were published in summary form in the *Osservatore Romano,* during the Synod of Bishops (October 1977); and the reports of the *circuli minores* in *Il Regno—Documenti* nos. 21 (1977) and 1 (1978). A synthesis relating to the subject of Christian initiation will be found in Armando Cuva 'La liturgia al Sinodo dei Vescovi sulla catechesi' *Notitiae,* no. 140 (March 1978) pp. 135-141.

Michel Dujarier

Developments in Christian Initiation in West Africa

THE AFRICAN Churches have played a central part in the restoration of the catechumenate. Thanks to the firm and enlightened policies of Cardinal Lavigerie, the last ten years or so have seen the re-introduction of the early Christian discipline of phased initiation of converts. This has meant that a serious, step-by-step process of instruction, with definite thresholds, has given the sacraments of initiation back their progressive character, marking stages of commitment to the Christian life. This progress still lacked one essential element: the ceremonies of bestowing a crucifix or medal to mark each stage of progress in conversion lacked liturgical status.

The re-introduction of baptismal stages was therefore greeted with joy, and immediately inspired a new quest for better teaching in the catechumenate. For the past fifteen years, the Churches of West Africa have been making many definite efforts in this sphere.[1] I should like here to describe the main principles underlying these, starting with an examination of the renewal of Christian initiation within catechumenal groups properly so-called, then going on to consider the new perspectives opening out beyond these groups.[2]

I. CATECHUMENAL GROUPS

The present renewed impetus given to the catechumenate stems from a programme of cultural research affecting initiation in its aims, teaching process and liturgy.

57

(a) The aims of Christian initiation

These have been influenced by three realities deeply enshrined in the African way of life:

1. The most obvious is the practice of *initiation ceremonies,* described in a multitude of studies.[3] These show how the pastoral question of Christian initiation can be seen in relation to traditional customs—which the Council and the new Ritual allow as part of Christian rites, with limitations and under certain conditions. Theologians and pastors both reject a facile concordism, superficially re-using certain rituals, as they do attempt to bring disused rites back into use. They are looking rather for basic approaches that would help create a new form of initiation suitable to the context of Africa today.[4]

2. Their quest naturally takes them beyond a study of initiation on its own, which is only a step, or series of steps, on man's journey from conception to the next world. Existence is seen and felt as a continuous process of growth, punctuated by rites signalling the crossing of the most important thresholds: birth, puberty, marriage, death. It is not the sum total of these moments, but a whole life, always one and the same life, but one growing in maturity and personalisation by gradual stages till it reaches its full realisation.

The *stages of life,* and the rituals surrounding them, are therefore receiving increased attention. The human person is a future in the unceasing process of being formed, and it is onto this process of maturation that the life of the Spirit must be grafted—a life that is likewise in itself a demand for growth to perfection. So the initiation of catechumens should bring them into the ambit of the history of salvation, consisting of progress and implying responsibility. The African concept of the 'strong times' of life is an excellent foundation for the concept of existence as an ascent to God. The convert who has experienced this journey through stages during his catechumenate is better equipped, once he has been baptised, to live the Christian life as a continual advance.

3. This advance is not carried out in isolation; the individual is formed *in and by the community* in which he lives. In his vertical relationships, he is part of a family with its own origins and customs: he defines himself by his attachment to this source and participation in these traditions; in his horizontal relationships, he is vitally linked to those who surround him, in bonds of giving and receiving.

This vital link with the community is particularly noticeable in the sphere of education, which becomes the task of the whole group, enabling Christian initiation to become effectively the responsibility of every member of the church group. On a broader canvas, the continual growth of each member of the community in the Spirit is made possible by the participation of each member in the life of the community.

So the process of Christian initiation rests on the three cultural supports of initiation rites, stages of life and the community link. Even if somewhat shaken and distorted by modern conditions, they still remain solid foundations on which to build a truly African Christianity, while being enriched in their turn by the vitality of the Gospel.

(b) The teaching process of Christian initiation

This is undergoing a radical revision of method as it comes to take these three supports into account.

1. We no longer speak of 'instruction', but of *tradition,* handing on. This, on the lines of Deut. 6, happens in the bosom of the family, of the group, of the community, as an experience lived and shared, celebrated and explained.

So, for example, in Bariba the first announcement of the Message is made by criers in the village assemblies. Among the Mossi, precatechesis consists of a presentation of the life of Jesus in song, a true celebration of the Christian epic. From then on, biblical texts set to rhythmical patterns are memorised more by assimilation than by learning.

2. We are trying to get away from any schoolroom atmosphere still attaching to catechumenal groups, reverting to an *initiatory* form of teaching, based on the life of the group, with everyone taking an active part. It is no longer a question of learning a lesson, but of learning to live, through dialogue and action.

In the diocese of Diébougou, for example, the catechumenate for children has developed along quite novel lines, with successive stages, each of ten days per month, in which young people from the villages come to learn the meaning of the Christian message, community and action through direct experience.

3. More radically, we refuse to let the catechumenate become something set apart. We want the church community to re-discover its *maternal* role. Christian initiation is not a separate process from the Church, nor even a special service within the Church; it is the *Church herself performing her maternal function.* This is something she can only do if all the baptised feel responsible for the education of their brethren, not just through example, but through their effective participation in the various ministries of the word, prayer and service. This is what teams of young people have been trying to achieve for eight years now in the larger towns of the Ivory Coast: catechumens and baptised together undertake a progressive discovery of the Gospel in small groups living and reflecting together, and regularly meeting other groups in the area so as to experience a wider community.

(c) The liturgy of Christian initiation

This too has become the object of concentrated research. The possibilities opened up by the new Ritual have led to numerous attempts to create African rites. These concentrate particularly on liturgical progress (stages), liturgical acts (rites) and the vocabulary of the liturgy (expression of faith).

1. Most dioceses have now adopted the *overall structure* of the Ritual, but with particular emphases:

The accomplishment of the different stages is being placed more and more in a setting of initiation: choice of place, vigil celebrations, intensive periods of meetings, particularly during Lent.

Within the limits allowed by the Ritual, 'rites of passage' are celebrated to mark the progress of catechesis and conversion during the years of catechumenate. The rite of anointing is sometimes included in this process. More often, the 'traditions', handings over, of the Pater and the Credo are enacted in solemn fashion.

Community participation is always regarded as an essential element in the ceremonies. The baptised are not content with being merely present; they intervene actively with singing, acclamations and dialogue. The community involvement is heightened by the part played by catechists, godparents and other lay people holding positions of responsibility.[5]

2. Certain rites that have particular *expressive value* in relation to local customs are carried out with their full richness of symbolism.[6] To give a few examples:

Among the Mossi, the rite of salt regains its full value at the entry into the catechumenate: each catechumen takes a handful of salt from a basket offered to him, and this is used in the *agape* following the ceremony. In other parts, converts are received by being handed the calabash of water that politeness requires be offered to a visitor entering the house.

The ceremonies of traditions or handings over and scrutinies are celebrated with a participatory fervour enhanced by the strength of feeling already attaching to the handing on of moral values and the victory over evil spirits. The initiatory texts proposed for the diocese of Bobo-Dioulasso are the Prologue to St John's gospel, the Beatitudes and Paul's hymn in praise of charity.

During the paschal vigil, the symbolism of death and resurrection is intensely expressed in a vivid ritual. Baptism is conferred in a sort of hollow tomb dug in the ground, or in a baptismal pool filled with water to thigh level.

3. In the field of *liturgical language,* the quest for a better means of expression is harder, but no less important.[7] Three aspects are involved: vocabulary, literary genre and world picture.

The key words of the Bible, of catechesis and of the liturgy play an essential part in understanding of the realities of faith. In many languages a particular effort is being made to revise religious vocabulary.

Besides words, an effort is also being made to make use of local literary genres. A literal translation from the Latin will not be understood: the idea behind it has to be expressed, and this requires original literary composition using the modes of expression proper to each local language.

At a deeper level still, each culture has its own world picture, which has to be assimilated if it is to be transformed by the Gospel. For example:

Exorcism has a particularly important part to play in demonstrating the victory of Christ and freeing the converted from the pressure and fear of spirits;

The experience of the Church as a family has to be given an appropriate form of expression and liturgical embodiment.

All this shows the main lines we are working on. The task is far from being finished. It will, of course, never be finished. But it has been undertaken with determination, courage and foresight, and we are already experiencing the joy of witnessing the first fruits of what promises to be a rich harvest for our local churches and the universal Church.

II. WIDER IMPLICATIONS FOR THE CATECHUMENATE

The fruits of this quest for a more vital, more communitary process of initiation, one more deeply rooted in local culture, can be found outside the catechumenal groups themselves. They amount to a new educational slant that is changing our whole pastoral approach. I would like to look at three fields in which a beneficial renewal is already visible:

Christian education of those who were baptised as infants;
Continued formation of the newly-baptised;
The ecclesial status of converts who cannot be baptised.

(a) *The education of those baptised as infants*

Here, chapter IV of the new Ritual opens up a rich vein of possibilities.[8]

1. The pastoral problem posed by infant baptism is the education that should be given after baptism. It applies both to adults who have never had any catechesis in their childhood, and to baptised children who come to us for catechesis. Psychologically, they are in a difficult situation: though baptised, many of them have had no initiation into the Christian mystery. Their faith has to be awakened, though they tend to fall passively back on the sacrament they have received; they have to be helped to progress in faith when they cannot easily see any reason for doing so.

2. Faced with this situation, we invite them to experience a true catechumenal course, alongside their non-baptised brethren, following

together the same catechesis and experiencing the same liturgical stages. Of course, as they are already baptised, the rites are somewhat different for them, but they follow the same course as those for the catechumens. By going through the stages with them, they make a personal discovery of what they have already received and can make a personal expression of commitment to the faith they are progressively discovering. So, in some dioceses, they celebrate their first Reconciliation in the same service of scrutiny at which their brother catechumens are exorcised. They receive their first communion, at which they renew their baptismal vows, at the same time as the catechumens are baptised.

This approach has certainly been a source of renewal, especially for the catechesis of children baptised as infants, which becomes a vital, progressive and communitary initiation, in which parents and godparents play an active and fruitful part.

(b) *Progressive education after baptism*

The institution of a continued course of Christian education after baptism is the second field in which the restoration of stages in the catechumenate has had a beneficial effect. The course initiated before baptism is, in effect, continued after it.

1. *The mystagogic period* is a first response to this need. We try to see it as an experience in perseverance in the brotherly life of the Church. The newly-baptised are invited to form teams to give each other mutual support in their growth in Christian life. With the help of their elders, they organise themselves into widely varying groups with great future promise.

2. More generally, *all the baptised* are thereby drawn into a movement of continual development. Besides the continuous formation of their faith, they need to foster their commitment: the dynamism of the base communities depends on this. This would be helped by a revitalisation of the renewal of baptismal vows during the Easter vigil, seen as the stage that all members of the community go through together, once a year, on their journey towards the Kingdom of God.

(c) *The status of non-baptisable converts*

The particular problem of converts who cannot be baptised is also partially solved by the restoration of the title of 'catechumen' in the Church.[9]

1. A common situation is for converts who have accepted the Word of God with faith to find themselves in a family or matrimonial *situation* that prevents their access to baptism. Since this is through no fault of their

own, and since they are effectively converts, we welcome them to the liturgical rite of entry to the catechumenate and carry on with their religious education.

2. They cannot be baptised, but their status as 'catechumens' binds them to the Church. They have the benefit of the support of the ecclesial community, as well as the blessings of the catechumenal rites. They devote themselves to the Lord and to their brethern in a life lived in the spirit of the Gospel. Their course and development are helped by the Spirit, even if they cannot be admitted yet to the sacraments of initiation.

These pages are a simple account of a quest that is going on, in the consciousness of how long it takes to bring about renewal, and particularly to bring new creations into being. But there is hope, shown in the astonishing vitality of young communities anxious to give the Church's mission as mother a more authentic embodiment. We share this hope with the Churches of the whole world, to whom we hold out a brotherly hand in a gesture of sharing, a process that can only enrich us all.

Translated by Paul Burns

Notes

1. 'Devenir chrétien en Afrique: Recherche sur les étapes catéchétiques et liturgiques de l'initiation dans la communauté chrétienne' (1977) issued by the Catechetical and Liturgical Commission of West Africa (PO Box 149, Bobo-Dioulasso, Upper Volta). This, a report of the inter-State meeting at Kuomi in 1976, gives numerous examples of the process I describe in this article.

2. I will only be able to give limited examples, characteristic of the sort of work being undertaken.

3. *Inter alia,* the reports of the Catholic Institute of West Africa (PO Box 8022, Abidjan, Ivory Coast), and the four volumes of *Recherche et Liaison* produced by the Presbyteral Council of Dakar (Senegal).

4. Mgr A. T. Sanon will shortly publish a study of initiation. This will develop the ideas put forward in his earlier works: *Tierce Eglise ma Mère,* 2nd ed., 1977, (PO Box 149, Bobo, 1977); 'Aux sources de la naissance de l'homme chrétien', in *Spiritus* 52 (1973) pp. 49-66.

5. The Mossi Rite of Christian Initiation is an excellent example (Ouagadougou 1973); there is an account of this in J. Fedry 'Une expérience baptismale en pays Mossi', in *Spiritus* 52, pp. 84-97.

6. The Bulletin of the Catechetical and Liturgical Commission of West Africa, *Le Calao,* gives many examples of stages in the catechumenate, in its nos. 37ff.

7. I. de Souza 'La difficile recherche d'un langage africain de la foi: quelques

lignes diréctrices' in *Spiritus* 50 (1972) pp. 268-73. V. also the bulletin *Afrique et Parole*.

8. 'En quel cas peut-on parler d'un catéchumenat post-baptismal?' in *Le Calao* 28 (1974) pp. 5-11 and 29 (1975) pp. 36-42.

9. 'Qu'est-ce qu'un catéchumène? Recherche sur le statut du catéchumène dans l'Eglise', in *Le Calao* 25 (1974, 1) pp. 21-9, and 26 (1974, 2) pp. 11-19.

Giorgio Zevini

The Christian Initiation of Adults into the Neo-Catechumenal Community

INTRODUCTION

'THE TASK of proclaiming the gospel to the people of our time, who are moved by hope but often wracked with fear and anguish, is without any doubt a service rendered not only to the Christian community but also to all mankind' (*Evang. Nuntiandi,* 1). In accordance with this awareness of the Church and in reply to the Council's invitation to get to grips with people as they really are, that is to say, a Christian people to whom the Gospel has not been preached, and to relaunch the Church's mission to them (see Mt. 28:19-20), an attempt has lately been made at a meaningful and stimulating Christian initiation of adults: the *neo-catechumenate* or the *neo-catechumenal community*.[1]

I. HISTORICAL DATA ON THE NEO-CATECHUMENATE

The neo-catechumenal movement began in 1964 in Madrid among the Palomeras slum-dwellers, with the work of Kiko Arguello and a few lay people who had been called by the Lord to live the Christian gospel among the poor. The proclamation of the gospel to the 'humble' (see Mt. 18:1-14) and despairing slum dwellers gave rise to a catechesis combined with reading the Bible (see Jn. 17:3). In this first attempt an outline *catechetical synthesis* emerged, 'a potent kerygma which, to the extent that it reached the poor gave rise to a new reality: the *koinonia*'.[2]

These lay people were witnesses to a Word, which was joyfully received by such poor people and thus gave rise to a community, listening and

65

praying, and to a liturgy in which these sinful brothers blessed the Lord for the wonders that he was working in them. Within three years there arose a real *gestation process of faith,* a kind of catechumenate, which was gradually creating a Church and a fraternal community (see Acts 2:42-47), and made visible the astounding fact of love for enemies within the dimension of the cross.[3]

This life of poverty of the Madrid community, in an atmosphere of simplicity and brotherly love, became a sign which attracted to the faith people who were far from the Church. Some parish priests, amazed at the powerful action of the Holy Ghost, wanted the same experiment to be tried in their parishes. The proclamation of the 'good news' of Jesus crucified and risen from the dead, by means of a two-month period of catechesis, gave rise to new communities on the road to conversion.[4]

The successful experiment in Madrid soon spread to other dioceses in Spain.[5]

In 1968 the neo-catechumenate began in Rome with the preaching of a peripatetic team including Kiko Arguello and Carmen Hernandez.[6]

In spite of the inevitable difficulties due to lack of understanding and in spite of the novelty, the results were so good that soon the proclamation of the kerygma was carried on by other brothers and spread to more and more parishes, not only in Italy,[7] but from 1972, in Europe,[8] and the Americas,[9] and the other continents.[10]

A team of itinerant preachers was created consisting of both priests and laity, who temporarily left their original community to become servants of the gospel (Col. 1:23; Eph. 3:7). They set up a communal programme for the growth of the faith, both gradual and intense, to rediscover the riches given by baptism. Recently at the request of certain parishes in the Anglican Church and in agreement with the Catholic and Anglican bishops of the area, itinerant preachers have introduced the neo-catechumenate to their Anglican brothers in Australia and England, who have welcomed the preaching with great joy.

This essay does not attempt to give an overall survey of the neo-catechumenate because this risks over-generalising in too short a space. Instead I want to give an idea of what the neo-catechumenate is like from the inside, as it has developed over the years in the experience of many communities and attracting attention, because of its world-wide expansion, the doctrinal depth of its biblical theology and its importance for the ecumenical movement.

II. THE NATURE OF THE NEO-CATECHUMENATE

The neo-catechumenate is a programme of faith and conversion which goes on within the existing structure of the parish, in communion with the bishop and the parish priest, and the aim of which is to enliven the preaching of the gospel and the continuing religious education of adults. Although it welcomes supporters, its main aim is to reach those who have dropped away from the faith, in order to respond to the Council's invitation, in a practical way, to preach the gospel to a Christian people to whom the gospel has not been preached.[11]

The preaching takes place in small groups of thirty to forty people, of all kinds, differing in age, political views, social and cultural background. They are called to hear the 'good news' of the Lord Jesus crucified and risen from the dead, and set out on a journey of faith within the community. It is not a spontaneous group or a base community, or a movement or association of parochial spirituality; *it is a post-baptismal road to deep conversion, divided into stages, whose goal is to rediscover in its truth and fulness Christian life and to bear witness to God's love for the world*;[12] it is a practical attempt to revive in today's conditions the work done by the Church in the early centuries with its catechumens.[13]

It is a practical way of bringing the Council to the parishes and thus of 'rebuilding the Church in the present century in the history that we are living through now'.[14]

Thus these communities have as their mission to be sign and sacrament in the parish of the missionary Church: to open the way for the preaching of the gospel to those who have strayed, giving, in the measure in which faith grows, the signs that call their brothers to conversion (see Lk. 4:43).[15]

One of the first aims of this initiation in the faith is the formation of the community, the *ekklesia*. In the beginning the newborn community is very imperfect, because of the inadequacy of the response of its individual members to God's call to conversion (see Mt. 1:15). In the early years all communities experience difficulties in loving their brothers 'as I have loved you' (Jn. 13:34). But the group slowly grows in faith and charity and acceptance of the word (see Thes. 1:6; 2:13; Eph. 1:13; Gal. 1:21-5), so that inability to love becomes a motive force for constantly rethinking the faith, a loud and clear call to conversion, while the community mirrors the sins of its brothers. True love then begins to destroy their securities, and to mean death to self and going outwards towards others. At this level behaviour to others calls in question their whole existence in history as believers in Jesus of Nazareth who loved his enemies to the end (see 1 Jn. 3:14), died without resisting evil and was raised again by God as the only truth (see Jn. 14:6), the only Lord of history. Thus the neo-catechumenate is a gradual descent into the depths of the self, experiencing *kenosis* with Christ, being submerged in the waters of baptism and rising with him to a new life.[16]

Thus with the growth of faith and love in the communities, they manifest to the world the visible body of the risen Christ (see Eph. 4:11-13; 1Cor. 12:4-11, 27) with the signs of humanity (Jn. 17:21) and love (Jn. 13:34-5) and revitalise the parish whose members return to the faith of the Church.

III. THE STAGES OF THE NEO-CATECHUMENATE

The neo-catechumenate is a long road. It has six stages corresponding to the progressive growth of faith.

1. *The proclamation of the kerygma*

A team of catechists composed of a priest and several lay-people give, at the parish priest's invitation, a two-month course in kerygmatic catechesis, inviting people of every sort to attend by various announcements both within and outside the parish. The basic theme of their preaching is the proclamation of salvation through the paschal mystery: Christ died for us so that the 'old man' might die together with his sins, and rose again so that the 'new creation' might also rise in us by faith and bring us into communion with God and our brothers, including our enemies. This brief period offers to all the option of faith and concludes with the birth of the community. The catechists go home and keep watch from a distance over the new community they have launched. The catechists report that during this first stage they constantly witness the miracle of people who are so moved by their preaching that they seriously change their lives, and that the true proclaimer of the gospel is Christ himself, who calls, converts, loves the sinners, whose lives are beset by many family, social, economic, emotional and psychological problems.

2. *The pre-catechumenate*

After the formation of the community, the second stage begins which lasts about two years. During this period the community seeks to strengthen its faith and make it more genuine by hearing the word and celebrating the eucharist. Members meet twice a week: to celebrate the word by studying the Bible, and to celebrate the eucharist at the Sunday liturgy. These celebrations are prepared in turn by five or six people, who read the scriptures in the light of the Spirit (see *Dei Verbum,* 12). Once a month the whole community takes part in a day retreat, in which each shares with the others his own experiences in the light of the word of God. The object of this stage is to pass from a devotional and sentimental faith to a new way of looking at life and history, as the place in which faith is affirmed and realised, not just as an emotion but as daily living with Christ on a road directed towards a mission. It is a privileged period of *kenosis* and conversion (see Acts 2:37-8), in humility and self denial. Each person is invited to go down into the depths of himself, to drop all masks and let his life be lit by the word of God. After two years the precatechumens undergo a *first scrutiny* in order to pass into the catechumenate; they reflect on what is required to 'leave everything for the Kingdom', to 'carry the cross', to follow Christ in a more radical way (see Mk. 8:34), convinced that faith is not a morality or the fruit of human endeavour but a gift which God offers man by baptism and that for every member of the community the Church is like a mother who gives birth to her child in the faith.

3. *The passage to the catechumenate*

The community continues on the road to conversion on the triple basis of word-liturgy-community for two more years, but goes more deeply into the various stages of the history of salvation. Salvation is seen as freedom from enslavement, based on the gospel teaching about wealth under the triple aspect of work-love-money, with the conviction that the Lord frees his people and purifies them by the power of the word. The catechumens are surprised to discover that it is possible to change one's life, escape from the judgment of the law and turn to mercy. This stage is concluded by a *second scrutiny,* the definitive passage to the catechumenate, in which the idols of the world are renounced publicly before the bishop so that God may reign at the centre of one's life: 'Whoever of you does not renounce all that he has cannot be my disciple' (Lk. 14:33; 12:33).

4. *The catechumenate*

During this period the community, still under the guidance of catechists, tries to achieve simplicity of life. They try to refuse the world's logic and abandon all compromise with evil. During the catechumenate, faith is a struggle in which the action of the liberating Spirit of Christ is felt. This stage lasts three years. First there is an initiation into prayer, the first weapon in the struggle, through the *Psalms.* Then comes the striving for a more robust faith through reflection on the *Apostolic Creed*; the *traditio et redditio symboli* is not an intellectual activity but a receiving of this Creed to restore it to the Church in the flesh.[17]

Finally, there is a second initiation into prayer through the *Our Father,* which is the heart of the gospel. Now the catechumens proclaim the word in their lives and announce it directly by visiting families in the parish. The Lord begins his work of inner simplification within the catechumens.

5. *Election*

The passage from the catechumenate to election is the stage of deepened catechesis. During this period the chosen are required to be a sign of God's love for men and to live a spiritual life of permanent 'eucharistia', offering their lives for the world in a spiritual and rational service.[18] The gate is narrowed. After so many years of striving, the demands of Christian living become natural and not forced. Within the catechumenate the reality of these demands has already been experienced constantly, God is choosing his own for a great mission: being a Christian.[19]

6. *Renewal of baptismal promises*

This is the last stage when people rest on the rock which is Christ and are confident in the power of the Lord. The catechumens live their daily spiritual lives joyfully with God and in expectation of the heavenly country. They are believers who have made the risen Christ the only Lord of their lives and realise that the various fruits of baptism are all free gifts from God, which the Church in all ages proclaims and revives today through the practice of the catechumenate.[20]

IV. THE FLOWERING OF MINISTRIES

The Second Vatican Council stated that 'the Holy Spirit unites the Church in communion and in the works of ministry, instructs it and guides it with various hierarchical and charismatic gifts, and embellishes it with its fruits' (*Lumen Gentium* 4). The rise of the neo-catechumenate has demonstrated a new structure of the local church formed by small communities, in which as faith grows, new charismata and ministries appear. Besides the *presbyter-parish priest,* the leader with the primary responsibility for the life of the community and its growth in the faith, there has arisen the ministry of the *responsible laity,* who serve their brothers and make present Christ the servant as a sign of service to the world, to which the whole community is called, by the preaching of the word, the service of the liturgy and by charity. For the service of the gospel there have also arisen the charismata of the *local catechist* and the *itinerant preacher,* called to give an account of our common hope in Christ. In particular the latter leaves his family, job, security to preach the gospel in other parishes and bear witness to the community that God alone suffices.Other charismata have also followed: those of the *singer,* the *reader,* and the *doorman.* Then there are two services connected with the needs of the community: *widows,* elderly women who entertain in their houses with Christian love the itinerant brothers in need of hospitality after a period of preaching the gospel and the *teacher* who helps to educate the community's children in the faith and the life of the community. This initiation into the faith stirs the people of God through various charismata and ministries to be the Church—community-communion united in the breaking of bread and the hearing of the word.

V. THEOLOGICAL FOUNDATIONS

We shall now try to sum up the theological framework within which the neo-catechumenal community operates.

1. *God's word as event*

The neo-catechumenate arose as a response to and acceptance of the kerygma of Jesus crucified and risen from the dead, and for it the word of God is primary. The initiation into the word is an amazing process: it is slowly read, meditated on in faith and then lived by in the community. The approach to the word is not intellectual but seeking wisdom, not speculative but prayerful. In fact for the neo-catechumenate the word of God is a reality, a force which creates and directs history, it is both event and action (see *Dei Verbum* 2). What is sought after is the word of life, how to hear and do it, what is required of us by God; not an ideology or raising of consciousness. The word is not something but someone, a person who speaks and throws light on our lives. Living by the word means surrendering to the power of Christ in our lives, being guided by him (see Rom. 10:17) and invited to see our own life-history and the community's as the history of salvation, convinced that community is created when God's intervention in our own lives is accepted and shared with our brothers in faith. This community of the Church becomes the organ capable of a saving re-reading of the word in the world today.

2. *Eucharist as the Lord's Passover*

At the heart of the neo-catechumenate stands the eucharist, the mystery of the Lord's Passover, through which the Holy Spirit reveals the whole economy of salvation and preparation for the fulfilment of all things. Here the community joyfully encounters the Lord's Passover which overcomes misery and sin; here it receives the reviving strength of its mission and becomes a sacrament of salvation for mankind and a sign of God's absolute love (see Jn. 3:16). These communities based on the eucharist are nourished at the two tables of the word and the body of Christ. They have found the deepest joy and centre of their lives in the celebration of the great Easter Vigil (see Ex. 12:42), which lasts till the rising of the 'morning star' (see 2 Pet. 1:19). During this night's vigil the catechumens see God's Passover in Jesus, the body of sin dies on the cross, the power of death is destroyed and by Christ's resurrection their own lives too are saved. Thus the neo-catechumenate goes from eucharist to eucharist, from Passover to Passover until the final Passover when Christ in glory will recapitualate all things in himself. It is important to stress here how this is a way of gradual initiation into the sacraments, a remaking of the inseparable link between the proclamation of the word and the celebration of the sacrament, between faith and sacramental practice.

3. *Accepting the glorious cross*

What enables one to travel this road is the strong conviction that the cross stands at the heart of the gospel. The whole of Christ's life tended towards the cross and his disciple must accept it in his own life (see Mk. 10:32-4; Lk. 12:50). For the catechumen proclaiming salvation today means proclaiming Christ's glorious cross and helping men to realise the truth about their own lives, with their limitations, alienations, unhappiness and inability on their own to give them meaning and then proclaim the victory that Christ alone has won through his cross. Selfishness is the cause of all human unhappiness. Proclaiming salvation in 'Christ crucified' (1 Cor. 1:23) means proclaiming the possibility of a new and different life and that God's glory is manifested in 'Yahweh's suffering servant' who does not resist evil and loves his enemies (see Is. 42:1-7; 49:1-6;50:4-9; 52:13-53, 12). The cross of Jesus reveals to every man that he is dead because he leads a life of selfishness which kills himself and others. Thus accepting the cross means accepting Jesus the servant as the one and only truth, because there exists no philosophy, politics or science by which mankind can be saved. The community living by this attitude of Christ becomes a sign for the world of God's love and proclaims that this love is always marked by the cross and that love can only be authentic and active in the world in and through the cross of Christ.

CONCLUSION

The renewal of the Church today is in some ways a return to the experience of the early Church and in particular the period of the catechumenate.[21]

In the last ten years the return to the catechumenate in traditionally Christian countries had developed into an important element in the

Church's pastoral evangelising mission.[22]

The post-conciliar Church in its consideration of the spiritual needs of people in today's socio-culture has come to certain conclusions: the priority of preaching the gospel over the administering of the sacraments in authentic Christian conversion, the local church as responsible for the word of salvation, the presence of small church communities in missionary situations, capable of stimulating growth in the faith by means of a catechumenal process within the structure of the parish. The neo-catechumenal communities have a strong sense of belonging to the Church and are aware that they are acting out the Church's mystery in themselves in response to the voice of the Spirit, which through Vatican II called the people of God not just to an 'updating' but a radical 'conversion'.[23]

We think that the neo-catechumenate, which renews the parochial structure as a community of communities, not only helps to cope with the crisis of a secularised Church and the crisis of personal authenticity in the split between 'practising' and 'lapsed' Christians, but also and especially helps in the Church's pastoral work of preaching the gospel. The neo-catechumenate is adapted to the rhythm of life today and is a practical and valid way of rebuilding the Church and the 'civilisation of love',[24] offering a road to conversion for sinners and preparing a home for the growth in faith of modern man.

Translated by Dinah Livingstone

Notes

1. For further information on the neo-catechumenate, see G. Zevini 'Le communità neocatecumenali. Un pastorale di evangelazzione permanente' in A. Amato (ed.), *Temi Teologico-Pastorali* (Rome 1977) pp. 103-125.

2. K. Arguello 'Le communità neocatecumenali' in *Riv di Vita Spir.* 2 (1975) 192.

3. *Ibid.,* 193.

4. *Ibid.*

5. In Spain today the neo-catechumenate is spread throughout 317 parishes of 30 dioceses with 693 communities.

6. At present there are 150 communities in Rome, 10 of which are in the parish of the Canadian Martyrs, the first parish to welcome the new idea and now the diaconal centre of the catechumenate.

7. In Italy there are about 1,000 communities in 506 parishes of 132 dioceses.

8. In Europe excluding Italy there are 838 communities in 404 parishes of 66 dioceses.

9. In the Americas there are 692 communities in 347 parishes of 95 dioceses.

10. In the other continents there are 64 communities in 48 parishes of 23 dioceses.

11. *Enchiridion Vaticanum* (Bologna 1968); SC 64 (115); 66 (117); 71 (123); 109 (194-6); LG 14 (324); CD 14 (604); PO 5 (1,253); 6 (1,260).

12. See 'Dopo il Battesimo' Pope Paul in *Oss. Rom.* (13 January, 1977).

13. See A. Laurentin & M. Dujarier 'Catéchuménat. Données de l'histoire et perspectives nouvelles', *Vivante Liturgie* 83 (Paris 1969); C. Floristan 'Teologiá y acción pastoral' *El Catecumenato* 1 (Madrid 1972); G. Groppo 'Itinerario di maturazione nella fede a dimensione catecumenale' in *Catechesi* 43 (1974/7) pp. 33-49, 62-3.

14. Paul VI 'La fede e la base per construire la Chiesa' in *Oss. Rom.* (15 July, 1975).

15. K. Arguello *op. cit.*, 195; Paul VI *Evangelii Nuntiandi*, p. 14.

16. K. Arguello 'Il neocatecumenato' in *Riv. di Vita Spir.* 1 (1977) 98.

17. *Ibid.*

18. *Ibid.*, 100.

19. *Ibid.*, 101.

20. *Ibid.*

21. See A. Laurentin & M. Dujarier *op. cit.*, 11; C. Floristan *op. cit.*, 16-31.

22. See *Ordo Initiationis Christianae Adultorum* (Typis Polyglottis Vaticanis 1972); see also J. Vernette & H. Bourgeois *Seront-ils Chrétiens?* (Lyons 1975); R. Falsini *Iniziazione Cristiana, Problema della Chiesa de Oggi* (Bologna 1976).

23. See *Enchiridion Vaticanum op. cit.*, LG 15 (325); GS 43 (1,459); UR 7 (522).

24. Paul VI *op. cit.*

Henri Bourgeois

The French Experience
in the Past Twenty Years

FRANCE is regarded as a traditionally Christian country, although thirty
years ago one question that was often asked was: Is France also a
missionary country? What is the situation now? And how can these two
different interpretations help us to assess recent research that has been
done in France into the process of initiation into Christian faith?

I. A CHANGE IN THE NATURE OF THE PROBLEMS

A survey made at the end of 1977 showed that there was a considerable
number of baptised adults in France. Out of a sample of 1,000 persons
questioned, 96% said that they were baptised. Of these, 82% said that
they were Catholic and 3% said that they were Protestant.

We should not, however, be deceived by these figures. This great
number of children baptised has raised the urgent question of initiation
into Christian faith. After all, not everything is achieved by baptism
alone. Baptism itself does not necessarily lead to effective membership in
the Church. And this gap between the sacrament and faith is something of
which many French Christians are painfully aware and which some of
them at least attribute to the failure, absence or ineffectiveness of religious education. This has led to many attempts to renew catechetics (by, for
example, M. Fargues, F. Derkenne and J. Colomb).

At about the same time, the same problem was also considered from
the point of view of baptised adults, since it is clear from the post-war
attempts to missionise France that the work of evangelisation at that time
went far beyond the religious education of children. It was within this
context that the catechumenate was once again set up in France—in

Lyons in 1953 and nationally in 1964. In this way, research into Christian education had two different but complementary focal points.

From 1968 onwards, our experience and our knowledge have, on the basis of certain facts, become much deeper. In the first place, there has been a fall in the number of child baptisms. Whether we are sorry to see this happen or whether we think of it as an improvement in the situation, we cannot afford to ignore it. In 1958, 91·7% of newly born children were baptised. Ten years later, in 1968, only 82·7% of such children were baptised—a fall of almost 10%.[1] What is more, it has been pointed out that fewer children have been enrolled since 1968 into groups for religious education. There is less pressure from families and attendance is less regular week by week. There are also many other activities of all kinds which claim the attention and the time of children, so that religious education is often thrust aside.

At the same time, certain new phenomena have made their appearance among adults in the past ten years or so. One of the most important of these phenomena has been the significant increase, both quantitative and qualitative, in the conversions of young adults, most of them, but not all, already baptised. Sects have been enjoying considerable success in France. Charismatic and Pentecostal forms of Christianity are flourishing. Those undergoing various forms of instruction have high expectations. All this points to the emergence of a new situation and calls for a re-examination and a redefinition of Christian education. We may sum up this situation by saying that there are at present fewer children being presented for baptism and religious education, but more adults presenting themselves for initiation into the Christian faith.

II. A COMPLEX OF MEANS FOR CHRISTIAN INITIATION

A recent number of the journal *La Maison Dieu* was, significantly enough, devoted to 'Christian initiation'. This phrase has come to be used more and more widely in France since the Second World War for the process of religious education generally. Its fundamental meaning is that Christian faith and life cannot be communicated simply as knowledge, but only as an experience. Christian initiation, in other words, is not simply religious instruction—it is an overall process. One becomes a Christian by a complex of coherent and orientated means.

1. *An Organic Complex of Means*

It is indisputable that initiation into the Christian mystery is bound to take place through knowledge of God's dealings with man in the past, since what he did during the period of revelation is the guarantee of what he is doing today and will do in the future. Religious education or catechetics are therefore not simply of secondary importance in the process of Christian initiation. It is clear, then, that the knowledge that is acquired in this process cannot be reduced to popular theological formulae or abstract statements.

Can it be restricted to biblical and liturgical knowledge? Can it be imparted by active methods? Experience has shown that what is involved here is an initiation at a much deeper level. The Christian message is handed on by people. It involves personal relationships, a mutual exchange of witness and words. It does not set some up in an active position, as teachers, and others in a position of passivity, as receivers. Everyone speaks and everyone listens and in this way the message is communicated to everyone.

The word 'catechism', then, has been replaced in the context of this widening of understanding by the term 'catechesis'. The first word, which was commonly used in the past, points to the practice of repeating and memorising a specific content of learning. The second points to an action in which several actors take part. It was common to hear French Christians talk, a few years ago, about religious education, using such words as 'sharing', 'dialogue' and 'expression', which emphasise much of what takes place in modern catechesis, both with children and with adults. Those who participate in it have repeatedly expressed the wish that there should be more and more 'free and welcoming areas', as they were termed at the Second National Assembly in 1973, where the Word could be expressed freely, outside the framework of the catechetical process in the strict sense of the word, in an industrial and post-industrial society in which many people lack the words to express their convictions, fears and hopes.

In recent years, there has been a certain reaction, noticeable in the reappearance of several concerns that had previously been reduced to a minimum. One of these is the serious problem of the content of religious education, in other words, of Christian objectivity and resistance to the risk of subjectivity. Another is the question of the use of memory in Christian initiation. Many Christians are claiming, not that we should return to mechanical memorisation, but that the positive values of recollection and meditation should be stressed in religious education.

In any case, what is quite clear is that Christian education cannot rely exclusively on pure knowledge. Other means have also to be employed—group work, celebration and links with everyday life, for example. These means were not disregarded by the earlier catechetical processes. They have, however, been given a new and vital part to play in modern Christian education. We will look more closely at each of these three elements.

In the first place, a great deal of emphasis has been placed on the educative work done in *groups* in recent years. Here too, the terminology used is significant. Just as, for example, catechism has been superseded by catechesis, so too does the catechist now tend to call him or herself an 'animator'. This animator listens sensitively to the words and the Word as it is formed within the group, because it is the memory of the group's past and bears witness to the faith of the Church. Because of this, initiation into the gospel is at the same time an initiation into the Church. The Church is not simply added to faith—it is the initiating form of faith.

The second element in the catechetical process is *celebration*. In the religious education of children, young people and adults in France today, a great deal of use is made of symbolic actions expressing, gathering together and even anticipating the search made by individuals and groups. For some years now, these celebrations have played a very special and valuable part in religious education. Christian groups and communities have learnt how to express their faith as and where it is through these celebrations, which are not fully sacramental rites in the strict sense of the word.

Thirdly, a concern for *everyday life* has been an important means for Christian initiation. It throws light on the experience of those who take part in the educative process on the basis of Jesus' own experience. We can also confirm, to sum up, that French Christians have discovered that the gap between the older form of evangelisation of the Catholic Action type and the more recent form of catechesis as described here is not so great as was feared. Both have their special features, but both are equally concerned with everyday life and with the gospel as it has been handed down in the Christian tradition.

2. An Orientated Complex of Means

The various elements of contemporary religious education in France that are briefly outlined above are necessary, but they are not enough. This is clear from the fact that many Christian groups make use of these elements, but that these groups are not necessarily taking part in a process of Christian initiation.

We must, therefore, draw attention to another fact. For a process of Christian initiation to take place effectively, there must be a firm orientation in the complex of means used to discover the gospel. The relationships and celebrations of the group and its links with everyday life must, in other words, have a sense of direction.

In practice, this means first and foremost that the children, young people or adults in the groups must have made a personal request. No Christian initiation is possible without a certain wish for it. It is true, of course, especially at the beginning of the process, that this wish or request may well be ambiguous. In the case of adults, it may be based on a discovery of Christian faith, but not necessarily involve baptism. Whatever may be the case, the French experience in recent years has shown how important it is that the process of initiation into faith should be as well motivated as possible on the part of those who take part in it. It is simply not enough to have a vague interest in religion or to be subjected to pressure from one's family in the case of a child or young person. It has become quite clear that it is necessary to have 'spaces of welcome and freedom' existing before the process of initiation in the stricter sense of the word begins.

On the other hand, of course, this orientation on the part of the group depends to a great extent on the aim of the animator. This is not without its problems, since the animator's perspectives inevitably depend on his own education or his Christian experience. He will also be very aware of the stages in the progress of the group and the steps that he has to take. This awareness is essential if the group is to be stimulated to move forward. At the same time, however, this progress cannot entirely be programmed in advance. It cannot certainly be imposed by the animator, whose ability will, in such an event, soon be recognised by at least some members of the group as authoritarianism. His lack of respect for the real progress of the group may, in such a case, lead to his rejection.

In the last resort, this orientation that is so important in the process of Christian education depends on keeping a balance between the original wish or request of each member of the group, the result that emerges from the interplay between these various wishes and the aim of the animator.

III. FAITH AND CULTURES IN CHRISTIAN INITIATION

Over the past twenty or so years, more and more light has been thrown on the delicate and complex relationship between faith and culture or rather between faith and various forms of culture by the research that has been carried out in France into Christian initiation.

1. *Lack of Faith or Lack of Balance in Society?*

One of the results of the work done among children, young people and adults in the sphere of religious education has been that we have begun to ask ourselves whether we have not too easily called those whom the Church has been unable to initiate into faith—perhaps because it has not understood their feelings or their concerns—'non-believers'. We do not deny the existence of indifference to religion—that is indisputable—nor do we want to call people who do not believe 'believers'. In many cases, it is possible to attribute lack of faith to failure on the part of the Church. This is a phenomenon that has been brought to light by the movement of the catechumenate in France today.[3]

In fact, although the Church has in recent years shown considerable flexibility in its approach to individuals and groups and in speaking in different languages to different classes and social categories, it has had great difficulty in observing important social changes which have affected people's expectations of the Church. In practice, the Church offers a Sunday eucharistic framework (although all baptised people are not equally qualified to participate regularly or fully in this liturgy). It also contains a number of militant and highly developed groups, makes sure that children and young people are educated in faith and provides certain services (baptisms, marriages and funerals). But, however wide this spectrum of provisions may be, it is not able to cover the full range of contemporary human needs. These needs include, on the one hand, the opportunity to speak freely about one's experience and reactions without having to use the language of faith and, on the other, the possibility for already baptised adults to take part in a process of initiation starting at the very beginning, without any presupposition of an already existing faith or religious convictions.

Through the movement of the catechumenate, the Church is gradually coming to take these two needs into consideration in France. Among the baptised people who want to be married in Church or ask for their children to be baptised, there are some who show, if they are questioned about it, that they would like to discover or rediscover faith. Among the Christians whose faith is uncertain, there are always some who call themselves members of the Church, but find nothing in the established Church that can satisfy them. Many such people are very happy to take part in the celebrations and activities of the movement of the catecumenate.

2. *Christian Initiation and Social Problems*

It has become more and more obvious with the passage of time that Christian initiation cannot be restricted to childhood. It has to take place—or take place again—at every period of man's development in a society as unstable and as lacking in continuity as our own. Certain new problems are, however, raised by this extension of period covered and these are above all social or cultural.

The first of these problems is that of the length of the period of initiation. Initiation is inevitably a process with a certain continuity, but nowadays it is often extremely difficult for people to follow a fairly long process of this kind because they are involved in changes of employment and their place of residence and are unable to regulate their leisure time or control the risks to which they are frequently exposed. A lengthy period of Christian initiation is therefore in many cases less suitable than a short, intense preparation.

The second difficulty is connected with the question of the expression or communication of faith. Modern consumer society with its tendency to isolate us has made conformists of us all. How, then, are we to dare to say what we are looking for and what we reject in our everyday lives? This is not a simple question. Indeed, it is made more complicated by the fact that many of our fellow-men are not spontaneously inclined to express themselves openly to others in words. This has led to an increased interest in symbolic and bodily expression and in audio-visual methods.[4] What has become quite clear is that there is no magic formula for success. All of those who are involved in the process of Christian initiation have to be very alert to its demands and problems and to be constantly creative, if it is to remain a popular and successful movement.

The third problem that has arisen within the present social context is connected with the shortage of personnel to act as animators. In view of the continuing fall in the number of priests, there is a strong temptation to find an immediate solution and recruit and send people out with insufficient preparation. Christian initiation is something, however, that takes place over a long period and requires great care. Fortunately, lay people have been trained for the work for quite a long time already. Nonetheless, the movement is still encountering difficulty in recruitment and training.

3. Practice and Reflection

The social and cultural aspect of the process of Christian initiation has also been accentuated by the theological and pastoral thinking that has taken place alongside the praxis, mainly in conferences, courses, meetings and articles of various kinds.

One of the most striking characteristics of this theoretical reflection about religious education in France is that certain categories of thought that have shown themselves to be too systematic or too ideological have gradually been abandoned. For example, the notorious contrast between faith and life and the equally well-known distinction between faith, as a gift of God, and religion, as a human phenomenon, have both disappeared from the theological scene. In the case of the latter particularly, it has become clear that faith is always the result of religious conversion and that those who prophesied the end of religion and the advent of an irreligious or post-religious age had gone to work too quickly. Another contrast which has also proved in the long run to be harmful is that between the sacramental function of the Church and its work of evangelisation. A complete separation of these two aspects of the Church cannot be maintained in praxis.[5]

On the positive side, the reflective process that has taken place in recent years in France with Christian initiation as its object has led to a serious attempt to define more precisely the scope of the practical experience. In the same context, attempts have also been made to clarify the meaning of the community of faith, conversion to the gospel, the confession of faith and Christian celebration. From this complex of themes, I would like to select two questions which seem to me to be very important.

In the first place, there has been a widespread recognition of the fact that there are different levels at which one can belong to the Church. Many theologians have insisted on the pastoral need to reject the idea of 'all or nothing'. In practice, we have above all to take seriously into account the different requests made of the Church, not in order to let the demands of the gospel sink down into the troubled waters of opportunism, but rather in order to be able to make the Church's service of the gospel more varied. We must learn to recognise that the gospel always leads us to clarify and convert men's expectations.

In the second place, theologians have pointed again and again to the urgent need for coherence in pastoral work. It is important, they have rightly concluded, to rediscover the true meaning of the sacraments of initiation into Christian faith. This discovery must be made if the achievements made in the process of initiation are not to be rendered negative by a too hasty or a too restrictive application of the sacraments. With this in mind, there has been a great deal of discussion in recent years about baptism, especially that of infants. In many cases, it has been proved that a presentation or a welcome, in the form of a Christian celebration, of the child has been more appropriate than the administration of the sacrament of baptism itself. The sacrament of confirmation is also similarly under consideration, with the aim of deepening its meaning and place in the process of initiation in young people and adults.

Translated by David Smith

Notes

1. See J. Potel *Moins de Baptêmes en France. Pourquoi?* (Paris 1974).
2. *La Maison-Dieu* 132 (1977).
3. J. Vernette & H. Bourgeois *Seront-ils chrétiens?* (Paris and Lyons 1975).
4. P. Babin & M. McLuhan *Autre Homme, Autre Chrétien à l'Âge Électronique* (Paris and Lyons 1977).
5. See two reports made of the French Bishops' conference at Lourdes: *Eglise. Signe de Salut au Milieu des Hommes* (Lourdes 1971) (Paris 1972); *Construire l'Eglise Ensemble* (Lourdes 1976) (Paris 1976).

Ad Blijlevens

Rituals used in the Baptism of Children in the Netherlands— Texts, Experiences and Reflections

I WAS ASKED to write a report or bulletin on experiences in the Netherlands in connection with new forms of rituals for Christian initiation. After consulting the editorial board, I decided to impose radical restrictions on myself. The material that is available is so wide-ranging and complex that it would be impossible to deal with it satisfactorily in a single article. I shall therefore confine myself here mainly to rituals that have appeared in two instalments of the widely used loose-leaf binder for practical liturgy, the *Werkmap voor Liturgie*.[1] In considering this, we shall at the same time bear in mind that infant baptism must be seen as part of the whole of Christian initiation and that there has for some time been a great deal of confusion in the Catholic West about the three sacraments of baptism, confirmation and the Eucharist. The reader who is interested to learn more about this should consult other contributions in this number of *Concilium* and other studies.[2]

In this article, I shall outline the most important elements in rituals that seem to be important and, wherever necessary, state my own opinion with the aim of providing a general picture of what is happening in the Dutch and Flemish-speaking world in the sphere of baptismal celebrations. In the second part of the article, I shall provide a few marginal notes on the developments described in the first part.

I. RITUALS

1. The series opens with 'The Administration of Baptism', which was compiled by a group of vernacular liturgists in Amsterdam (the Werkgroep voor Volkstaalliturgie) and published, after it had been in use for some years in the student community in Amsterdam, in 1966 in one of the first instalments of the *Werkmap voor Liturgie*.

The celebration of baptism is impressively placed in this liturgy within the whole context of the history of man and his salvation: 'from creation to flood and Christ, through a long tradition of generations, to come to this community and this child in the community'.[3] The parents, the godfather and the godmother are all given an important part to play in this dynamic event.

What is of particular interest is the promise made by the parents. This or a very similar promise occurs again and again in later baptismal rites:

Do you promise to be a good father and a loving mother to your child?
Do you promise to give your child a Christian education and to bring him/her up in the spirit of the gospel?
Do you promise to remain faithful to your child, whatever the future may bring, and to respect him/her, wherever he/she may go, and to remember always that your child is born of God?

A striking aspect of this form of baptism is that the language used is emphatically biblical. A wide choice of material is provided for singing.

2. 'The Baptism of a Child' is the work of the group 'In the midst of you' (Werkgroep Midden onder U) working in Maastricht. It is similar to the first liturgy, but is more popular in form. It first appeared too in 1966.

The dynamism of the Church and the history of man's salvation emerges less strongly and the whole ritual is less cohesive than the first example. The parents and sponsors are placed firmly within a family framework. One remarkable feature of the liturgy is that the parents' promise is introduced by a reference to the marriage promise. Only one scriptural reading is provided. This is Mark 10: 13-16 (Jesus and the children). It is so closely integrated into the whole of the ritual that it is not possible to use another passage.

3. The 'Order of Service for Infant Baptism' published in 1968 by the Flemish Interdiocesan Commission for Liturgy (ICLZ) is to a very great extent based on the preliminary draft of the Roman *Ordo baptismi parvulorum*. It is, however, original and creative in several places. There are also very many symbols and ritual actions. Unfortunately, the fundamental meaning of baptism is not sufficiently stressed and the various elements are not clearly interconnected.

One advantage of this ritual is that it does make an attempt to stress the fact that it is a child who is being baptised. The parents and their responsibility for their child's upbringing are therefore given great emphasis. On the other hand, the part which they play is not sufficiently integrated into the role of the Church community. The exhortations addressed to the parents are, moreover, scattered all over the whole ceremony and the human element does not emerge very clearly.

4. Liturgists working in the University parish at Louvain compiled a practical celebration of baptism, *Werkboek voor een doopviering,* which was published in 1974 by the Apostolate for the Life of the Church at Westerloo in Belgium. In this service, baptism is integrated into the celebration of the Eucharist, taking its place immediately after the Service of the Word. The authors provide many suggestions for opening words, readings and songs. The whole baptismal service is very reminiscent of the Amsterdam liturgy (see 1. above), especially in the emphasis that it places on incorporation into the Christian community on the way and on the community's responsibility towards the child. The following text will serve to illustrate the quality of this liturgy:

> 'In the name of God, the children of Israel went out of Egypt to the Promised Land. In this exodus, they passed through the water of the sea and escaped from the clutches of those who had enslaved them. Water is therefore for us the great sign of being set free from captivity and of being born to new life. We appeared as a new people from the water of the sea. In the name of God, in the name of the Father and the Son and the Holy Spirit, I baptise you, N., so that you may belong to the people that passed through the water and became the free people of God'.

Compared with the Amsterdam example (1. above), this service has the great advantage of providing a choice of biblical readings, songs, prayers and models of homilies. This great choice is, however, also something of a disadvantage in that it weakens the unity of the rite as a whole.

5. In the first six editions of his book *In het voorbijgaan* (Utrecht, 1968-1972), Huub Oosterhuis published his baptismal rite 'Geboorte vieren'. The English translation of this book appeared in two volumes in 1970. 'Celebrating birth' appeared in the volume *Prayers, Poems and Songs* (New York 1970), which contains the text quoted below.

If we compare this liturgy with the Amsterdam service above, we notice at once that the ritual part has been radically shortened and weakened. The whole celebration is much simpler, but it is also less biblical and less closely associated with the history of salvation. This is especially clear from the omission of the part dealing with sin and death and the confession of faith. Two non-biblical readings have also been added, the second in connection with the use of the seven-armed candlestick. The 'story', as Huub Oosterhuis calls it, begins thus: 'As everyone knows, there are seven flames in the universe and together they form the air that we breathe and the ground beneath our feet—in a word, they comprise everything. But there are also seven flames in every person, because every person is a little universe and that is why there are seven candles burning on that candlestick.'

The seven flames symbolise the flame of the sun, the flame of language, the flame of passion, the flame of hunger and thirst, God himself, the flame of music and the flame of hope. In this way—and at the same time by means of candles held by the children present—the baptismal candle of the Amsterdam liturgy (1. above) is replaced and given a new meaning. On the other hand, the significance of baptism does not emerge very clearly in the ritual as far as the child is concerned. Its significance for the parents and the others who are present can be summarised in the words 'your child is born of God' and 'you must be born anew'.

6. In Dolf Coppes' 'Service of Infant Baptism', published in the fourth loose-leaf liturgical binder of 1970 (*Werkmap voor Liturgie* 4, 1970), only one of the symbolic actions used in baptism—the baptismal gesture itself—was retained. Coppes wanted above all to do justice to those who believed that baptism brought about no intrinsic change in the child. He therefore emphasised only the fact that the parents wanted to see the birth of their child in the light of God and the community of believers. He also took into account, in this liturgy, the attitude of those who wanted to keep that community of believers fairly universal. Two authors, De Grave and Geudens, correctly assessed Coppes' rite of baptism as 'an expression of the hesitations that prevailed in the Netherlands round about the year 1970. Many people felt then that many formulae and ideas were no longer valid and that there was too little sympathy for what was new. . . . We are bound to say to all those who are looking for a conscious community of Christians, to parish priests who are hoping, on the occasion of the baptism of a child, to give the parents a little insight into the nature of Christian freedom and community and to those who love symbolism: Look elsewhere. The theological implications of this rite we shall not consider in this context'.[4]

7. Gerard Lukkens' 'A Celebration of Infant Baptism' was published together with the three following liturgies (8, 9 and 10 below) in the *Werkmap voor Liturgie* 7 (1973). It is, from the theological point of view, much more heavily charged.

The symbolism of light is especially strongly emphasised in connection with baptism as a paschal event, as are incorporation into the community and the parental task of education. In this rite, the child is also given an important part to play, in regard to, for example, the place he or she occupies in the ceremony, the specially adapted readings from the Bible, the choice of songs and the general expression. Baptism takes place by means of immersion, during which the following closely related text is used: 'N., you are immersed in human existence, in the suffering of all of us, in the chaos, fear and conflict that surrounds us all. Yet God created the world good. He is our Father who preserves everything and brings everything to a good end. N., I baptise you in the name of the Father. N., you are immersed in the death of him who lives, even though he died, Jesus the Lord. His word and his love aroused expectations everywhere in the world. May his name be praised. Become a partner of those who are, in his name, building a better future. N., I baptise you in the name of the Son. N., be reborn through the breath of God's Spirit, the Spirit of Jesus, who unites what is divided, creates space and blows where he will—the Spirit in whom we live, move and are. N., I baptise you in the name of the Holy Spirit.'

This baptismal formula is always said by the president. The other texts are spoken in turn by the father, the mother and the godfather or godmother. The text quoted above may indicate something of the nature of the ritual, in which classical elements are used in a new way and contemporary feelings are expressed in a striking form.

8. In Jan Nieuwenhuis' *Ergens komt een kind vandaan* ('A child comes from somewhere'), baptism and the Eucharist are celebrated in the presence of the local Church community. Great emphasis is placed on the connection between being baptised on the one hand and rebirth and the community on the other. The role of the parents is, however, rather under-emphasised. The message of baptism is extended into the eucharistic prayer and there is a considerable choice of readings (both biblical and non-biblical), rites and songs.

9. Like Nieuwenhuis' rite described above (8), Huub Oosterhuis' *Als je kind je vraagt* ('If your child asks you') is also a baptism and celebration of the Eucharist in the presence of the local Christian community. The addresses in this ceremony are splendid. 'The first deals with opposition to the social structures of power and the need to create a world of love, in accordance with Jesus' ideas and life. The second is concerned with the need for freedom from all firmly rooted habits and for rebirth. The community of believers is described in a unique way as a group of people who, in the name of Christ and in imitation of him, is in contestation with the established order and its desire for war.'[5] The other texts in the service of baptism and the Eucharist have a rather more meagre content.

It is interesting to compare 1. the 'Administration of Baptism', for which Huub Oosterhuis was largely responsible, 5. 'Celebrating birth' and this ritual, 'If your child asks you'. Each is much more austere and economical than its predecessor. In the last, even the baptismal formula is absent. The eucharistic prayer is, however, adapted to the baptismal event.

10. In 'Ingredients for the celebration of a baptism', Fred Kessen has provided at least one splendid text based on the baptismal water: 'In the power of Jesus of Nazareth, we make ourselves responsible for N. and for every child on earth. We hope to be fresh water, waves of faithfulness who will bear them up. We intend not to be a poisonous environment for this child and so many others, not to be an inherited evil, a pool in which a child might choke to death. In Jesus' name, we ask the Father that we may be inherited grace, an environment of the good Spirit. May N. and all children play and grow in a sea of love, a sea of people, alive in the Spirit of Jesus'.

11. The Maastricht group 'Midden onder U' has provided, with 'I baptise you' a good alternative to the earlier 'Baptism of a child' (2. above). The theme of 'the way' plays an important part in this later liturgy and children are actively involved in the celebration. Another important element in this ritual is the stress placed on the parents' subjection to God. God's concern with the child to be baptised here and now and the part played by the child, the parents and—to a lesser degree, admittedly—the Church emerge quite clearly. On the less positive side, very heavy emphasis is placed on the ultimate impotence of the parents and on the child's responsibility with regard to his or her 'own way'.

12. The same group has also published 'Water, bread and wine', a service of baptism combined with the Eucharist and giving special attention to the question of integrating children into the celebration. It is essentially a domestic liturgy which is informal and adapted—in my opinion too much—to the needs of children. The catechetical element is also strongly—too strongly—emphasised.

13. 'Water and fire' is a service for children compiled by Harrie Wouters which was published in 1974 in the series *Werkcahiers voor vieringen met kinderen* (No. 5). It is so strongly orientated towards children that little attempt is made to integrate adults. The symbolism of water is strikingly expressed, although its significance with regard to Christian baptism does not emerge very clearly.

14. The last baptismal rite of the many that have appeared in Holland and Belgium in recent years which I would like to mention here is Piet Zoon's children's 'Baptism' (Hilversum 1977), which was published as a workbook (in the English sense of the word) for children. Many of the elements in this workbook providing stones from which the children have to build their own service of baptism are derived from rituals already described above. (An example of this is the ceremony of the seven flames—see 'Celebrating birth', 5. above.) A great advantage of this ritual is that each stone for building the service is accompanied by a short

consideration of baptism as an event: its origin, development, the theme of becoming man, the idea of mutual responsibility and baptism seen as the first step.

II. MARGINAL NOTES

A number of positive elements emerge clearly from our brief examination of various baptismal liturgies. A great deal of emphasis is given in many of the rites, for example, to the history of man and his salvation. The Church is also brought well to the fore and the parents and sponsors are given an important part to play. The connection between baptism on the one hand and the Eucharist and the Church on the other is also stressed and concrete possibilities are provided for giving form to this reality.

The attempt to compile good texts which are distinctively Dutch or Flemish, to present biblical teaching in a modern context, to renew the symbolism of baptism and to achieve a close unity between word and rite has led in many cases to rituals of a striking and authentic creativity. This creative effect is often heightened by the use of very suitable music. The more active involvement of children in these celebrations is also a positive achievement which makes the rite of baptism and its meaning more accessible to young Christians.

There are, however, also certain dangers that have not always been avoided in some of these rituals. I have already mentioned the rather one-sided orientation in several cases towards the local community and even towards the family circle. The great stress that is placed in many of these celebrations on the link between baptism and the Eucharist also contains an inherent danger—that baptism may lose its distinctive form and meaning and that the Eucharist may become even more over-emphasised than it is already and in this way become devalued. There is also a similar danger in the baptismal liturgy itself of giving too much emphasis either to the text or to the symbolism. It would be preferable to give more attention to the task of integrating both elements in the service. Both an intellectual and an emotional approach have a harmful effect on the celebration of any liturgy. The ideal service combines word and gesture in an indissoluble unity. The adage 'not many, but much' can certainly be applied to many of these liturgies, at least as a suggestion for their improvement.

Finally, if the process of adaptation to the needs of children is carried too far, it may lead to a degree of infantilism and a consequent neglect of the task of making the real meaning of Christian baptism clear to all those present. There is also a real danger that the baptism of a little child tends to be regarded too much as a *rite de passage* and too little as a real rebirth in Christ and his Church.

Certain aspects of these recent services of baptism are of great importance. One of these is the increasing use of what have come to be known as 'baptismal conversations'. In these, the priest and the parents together discuss the motives for baptism and reflect about the meaning of the sacrament and the whole question of responsibility that goes with it. The celebration itself is often discussed in these conversations. A selection is made of the material available and sometimes the whole or part of the service is compiled or at least outlined in principle. Another important aspect is that a great deal of attention is often given to the question of after-care. Many suggestions have been made about what can and should be done after the baptismal ritual itself in a number of publications.[6] One valuable practice is that of holding services in which children are blessed. These and other forms of involvement often take place at the weekend.

This practice must, of course, extend beyond liturgical forms and also beyond the very early years of the child's life. It is only in the strength of God's grace and in relationships with all those who in one way or another are responsible for the child that he or she, who was made a Christian in baptism, will become more and more deeply Christianised.

Translated by David Smith

Notes

1. *Werkmap voor Liturgie* 11 (1977), instalments 2 and 3. These instalments are devoted to the future of infant baptism. They include a series of contributions edited by G. Lukken. With regard to the rites discussed in this article, I am also indebted to the analyses made by my Flemish colleagues, R. de Grave and L. Geudens (pp. 110-145). The editor of these instalments worked on the assumption that a review of the present situation could not be restricted to a mere discussion of various orders of service. He therefore included contributions containing notes on the preparation for baptism, meditations on the symbolism of baptism, a concise theology of the sacrament, a discussion of baptism from the ecumenical point of view and suggestions for catechesis after baptism and celebrations with recently baptised children.

2. See, for example, G. Kretschmer 'Nouvelles recherches sur l'initiation chrétienne' *La Maison-Dieu* 132 (1977), pp. 7-32; English translation: 'Recent research on christian initiation' *Studia Liturgica* 12 (1977) pp. 87-106.

3. *Werkmap voor Liturgie* 11 (1977) p. 114.

4. *Werkmap voor Liturgie* 11 (1977) p. 129.

5. *Werkmap voor Liturgie* 11 (1977) p. 135.

6. *Werkmap voor Liturgie* 11 (1977) pp. 166-241.

Joan Estruch and Salvador Cardus

Baptism as Initiation: New Changes in its Meaning

THIS ARTICLE forms part of a wider study in which the authors are currently engaged, on the evolution of the rites associated with birth and death. The data on which this is based were collected in a field study carried out on the island of Minorca in the Balearics, and the study itself forms part of a wider research project, designed to examine Durkheim's assertion that religious matters are being transformed, as opposed to Marx and Freud's thesis that they are being abolished. It should, in the final analysis, advance the study of what Luckmann has called 'invisible religion', Towler calls 'common religion', and we would call 'new forms of religiosity', or—with obvious reference to Weber—the 're-enchantment of the world'.[1]

The purpose of this article is far less ambitious and far more specific. Its approach is threefold:

(1) We write deliberately from a sociological, not a theological, standpoint, so as to approach the subject matter from one particular angle. This has its limitations, but at the same time we would claim for it the necessary autonomy not to have to take 'the doctrinal elements of Catholicism as a theoretical category'.[2]

(2) We base our arguments on analysis of the material gathered in a field study of popular customs connected with baptism, and on an examination of the present pastoral approach of the Church to this rite. We start from the hypothesis (which analysis confirms) that in no small proportion of cases the view of baptism held by the parents—as 'customers'—is at variance with that held by many

91

priests, who view the meaning of the rite from the standpoint of the 'supplier'.

(3) The final purpose is to raise some questions, in the hope that a consideration of them will prove useful to theologians, liturgists and pastors.

I. AMBIGUITIES IN THE RITE OF BAPTISM

Birth provides an ideal occasion for analysis of ritual sequence; there is a real 'ceremonial of transition', embracing the rites of engendering and fecundation, pregnancy, birth and the period following, and of incorporation of the new-born baby. As Eliade says: 'baptism is essentially a rite of initiation', one of the last remaining traces in Western society today of the old mysteries of initiation.[3] But it has two dimensions, both of which need to be studied: at once a rite of dissociation and of association, baptism is partly a cleansing, a rite of purification, of separation from the world one starts from, and partly also a rite of incorporation and integration into society.[4]

Sociologically speaking, baptism as a rite of initiation and celebration of birth is not specific to the Judaeo-Christian religious tradition. It is a virtually universal phenomenon, much earlier than Christianity, which Christianity has both *adopted* and *adapted* so as to give it a particular purpose. The cleansing aspect of the rite is given a specifically Christian context of purification from the stain of original sin, while its integrating aspect becomes a means of incorporating the neophyte in the Church, making him a member of the communion of saints.

Despite its earlier origins, there is no doubt that historically it came to be part of the Church's monopoly in the administration of the rites of passage in Western society. To a large extent, this monopoly situation still holds good today: in fact one might say that the administration of the rites of passage is now the last bastion in which the Church still holds a monopoly position, as shown by the difficulties experienced—still—by civil society in finding workable and symbolically effective substitutes for the ecclesiastical rites of which baptism is such an important element. There are exceptions, but they prove the rule: there was the '*Namensgebung*' (name conferral), which in Nazi Germany succesfully supplanted Church baptism for a few years; Eastern European countries have tried to topple the Church from her monopoly position by working out State liturgies to fulfil the same functions. In the German Democratic Republic, the ritual formula used in the ceremony replacing baptism keeps a surprising resemblance to the Christian formulations on which it is clearly based. So the parents and godparents promise: 'We, parents and godparents, commit ourselves to bringing up this child in the spirit of peace, of universal friendship and of love for our country, so as to provide a happy future for him in Socialism'.[5]

Clearly, with a few exceptions such as the above, the Church's monopoly of administration of the rites of passage has the important consequence that, in most cases, baptism as a rite of integration into the Church also acts as a rite of incorporation into society as a whole. This produces a series of ambiguities necessarily reflected in some of the ambiguous attitudes of present-day pastoral practice, which we shall examine in due course.

II. THE TWO COMPONENTS OF THE RITE

The ecclesiastical ritual used to stress the first of the two components of baptism—cleansing and integration—to the detriment of the second. In Minorca,[6] baptism was formerly carried out immediately after birth, two or three days after at the outside. The only exceptions were babies born during Holy Week, who were not baptised till Easter so that they could benefit from the 'new water'—newly blessed and therefore more efficacious, a guarantee of future happiness. The reason for the haste was fear of the ever-present threat of death before the baby could be cleansed from the stain of original sin. The same reason meant that people other than the priest, particularly the midwife, were able to baptise at the moment of birth if necessary. The women who acted as midwives in the towns and villages of Minorca used to have to be 'examined' by the parish priest before exercising this calling, so that he could be satisfied of their ability to administer the rite correctly.

The same emphasis on the element of impurity affected the circumstances in which the ceremony was carried out. In view of the short interval after the birth, the mother was not present; she stayed in the house in which she had had the baby, from which she would not emerge for several weeks (usually forty days), when she went to church for the *benedictio mulierum post partum,* another cleansing rite which freed her from the state of impurity in which giving birth had placed her, and was an essential prerequisite for her reintegration in social life. So with the mother absent, the main feminine role at the baptism was taken by the godmother. But when the procession left the house for the Church, it was not she who carried the baby but the midwife, performing her social function of intermediary between society and impurity. All impurity carries the risk of contamination, so only the midwife could carry the baby, with the godmother walking on her right. After the ceremony, with the infant cleansed, the procession re-formed to return to the house, but now it was the godmother who carried the baby, and who received the congratulations of the neighbours.

Once back in the house, there was a party, and it was this that really demonstrated the integrating aspect of the rite. The party was presided over by the parents, though organised and paid for by the godparents. Family, friends and neighbours were invited, and given refreshments— the residue of the ancient ritual banquets used to solemnise the association of the new-born child with society. The survival of the custom of throwing sweets and titbits to the children in the street during the course of the party is another clear reminiscence of earlier ritual behaviour, showing that integration was effected at the level of the whole community.

<h2>III. THE EXPECTATIONS OF PARENTS AND PRIESTS</h2>

The dissociation of the ecclesiastical ceremony from the family and social celebration of a birth, which still persists, helped to strengthen the split between the two aspects—the cleansing and integrating aspects—of the rite of baptism, with the result that the baptism administered by the Church came to be associated almost exclusively with the aspect of purification from original sin.

In recent years, however, Catholic pastoral thought on the sacraments has evolved in the opposite direction—placing the stress very firmly on the integrating aspect of the baptismal rite. This means that there is now hardly any mention of original sin and of purification, and the integration side is very specifically made integration into the Christian community, not into society as a whole. From a sociological point of view this also gives rise to ambiguities. These can perhaps best be seen from an examination of the contradictory expectations of parents and priests.

Briefly, the problem stems from the fact that when parents ask the priest to baptise their infant, many priests do not automatically agree to do so, but set various conditions and require certain guarantees. We are not concerned here with priests who do not set any conditions, nor with parents who do not want their child baptised, nor with parents who fully satisfy the requirements set by the priest: the point at issue only arises when priests not prepared to baptise indiscriminately come up against parents who want their child baptised even though they cannot fulfil the conditions asked of them. At the risk of simplifying somewhat, these conditions can be summed up as a call for 'maturity in faith', without which the priest would rather delay baptism or deny it altogether.

In this situation, priests tend to rationalise the attitudes of parents by placing them in one of the following categories:

(a) many parents' attitude can be summed up in the phrase, 'I don't go to Mass, but I believe in "something" . . .';
(b) many non-practising Catholics who still ask for their children to be

baptised perhaps have something like, 'faith with deep under-
ground roots', 'unconscious faith', or even a sort of 'religious
instinct';

(c) they are only doing it because it is traditional, and because they see
     it as 'a right that cannot be denied them';
(d) they are doing it simply from 'social pressure', not from 'religious
     motives'.

Priests who tend to place parents in one of the first two categories end
up in favour of administering baptism despite everything, while those
most disposed to see parents acting from 'tradition' or 'social pressure'
are, logically, most resistant to doing so.

IV. THE DISADVANTAGES OF THE PRESENT SITUATION

There seem to be certain presuppositions underlying these rationalisations, particularly as applied to the last two categories.

The most obvious is a usually implicit, but sometimes explicit, criticism
of the 'consumer' approach of parents, who come to church to fill their
children with baptism in the same way they would fill their cars at a petrol
station. Even if this criticism is justified, and many people do approach
priests in this way, consciously or not, the attitude still raises various
questions. Such as:

(1) Is it not fairly natural that in a society constantly classed as
     'consumer-orientated' religious goods should come to be seen as
     one more class of consumer product?
(2) If the answer to the first question is in the affirmative, is it not
     reasonable to expect priests to accept the inherent contradiction,
     rather than require 'maturity in faith' of those brought up (by
     themselves or their forbears) in a way that makes this 'maturation
     process' most difficult?

Secondly, if one objects that what priests are doing is just pointing out
the anomaly so as to make people see their decision (to ask for baptism)
as a free act, not one conditioned by upbringing and tradition, then one
still has to ask whether the people should not come to this conclusion on
their own initiative, without being prompted. Are such 'promptings' (or
'conscientisations' in the current jargon) perhaps a new—admittedly
'aggiornato'—manifestation of secular clerocracy?

In the third place, remembering the Church's monopoly position in the
administration of the rites of passage such as baptism, the question of
'consumption' and the 'filling station' appears in a new light. If we may

pursue the petrol simile, we can say that it is one thing for a petrol company to refuse to supply customers who can easily go to a rival, but quite another for it to cut off supplies when it is in a monopoly situation and the customer therefore has no alternative source of supply. In the situation under discussion, the Catholic Curch is the State monopoly, not simply Shell, B.P. or Esso . . .

Underlying this matter of 'consumer approach to the sacraments' there would appear to be another, deeper, major factor to be considered. The priest's request for guarantees, in the form of what we have called 'maturity in faith', is really based on a fairly radical transformation—though this is not generally admitted—of the meaning of the baptismal rite itself. This has two symbolical aspects—cleansing and integration. What has happened now is that the former has virtually disappeared from ecclesiastical and pastoral considerations of baptism. Without going into the theological aspects of this (which we are quite unqualified to do), we can state as a fact that the theme of *original sin* does not fit in with modern thinking and that it is therefore difficult to give baptism its former character of cleansing or purification. This is why modern thought concentrates almost exclusively on the second, integrating, aspect of baptism. This, in the final analysis, is the justification for requiring 'mature faith' as a condition for incorporating the infant in the Christian community through the administration of the sacrament.

How has the present eclipse of the cleansing aspect of baptism come about? One view would be that the whole business of pregnancy and giving birth has come under the control of a group that at present enjoys greater prestige and credibility than the clergy: the medical profession.[7] The arguments employed by writers such as Szasz and Illich, though not dealing specifically with this point, would seem to support this thesis.

One can equally well ask, however, how far a society whose official ideological language exalts egalitarianism, a society that enthrones the *citizen,* in which lowly, sinful man becomes *free* man (in the official ideology) . . ., how far such a society can admit the concept of original sin. This is perhaps why the subject of sin is avoided by so many, perhaps why the Church of the *aggiornamento*—the Church adapted to such a society—has to deny (or at least keep quiet about) original sin.

CONCLUSION

Our conclusion is that the rationalisations made by priests of the attitudes of people who come to them asking for their children to be baptised, in fact hide a more important phenomenon: nothing less than a transformation of the meaning attached to the rite. This transformation has to be muffled or camouflaged for the good reason that it has not been doctrinally promulgated, but in pastoral practice it has nevertheless become a fact. So it does not seem unjustifiable to speak of ambiguities and contradictions in the pastoral practice of many priests today.

Without in any way claiming to have exhausted the problems surrounding baptism in the Catholic Church today, we hope we have raised some pertinent questions, and that they will be of some use to theological and pastoral thought.

Translated by Paul Burns

Notes

1. See T. Luckmann *The Invisible Religion* (New York 1967); R. Towler *Homo Religiosus: Sociological Problems in the Study of Religion* (London 1974). Our own work is slightly institutionalised at a centre of investigations into the sociology of religion: ISOR in Barcelona.

2. Jacques Maître 'Problèmes épistémologiques posés par une sociologie du baptême' in *Epistémologie Sociologique* 5 (1967) p. 399.

3. M. Eliade *Birth and Rebirth* (New York 1958).

4. These two aspects were first formally recognised by A. van Gennep in his classic study *Les Rites de Passage* (Paris 1909) pp. 90 ff.

5. Quoted by K. Richter 'Rites and symbols in industrial culture' in *Concilium* (Feb. 1977).

6. The case of Minorca should not be considered exceptional, but a particular example of a widespread phenomenon.

7. On the same level, we show in our wider study of the rites surrounding birth and death, how the ritual of 'churching' of women who have given birth (the *benedictio post partum*) fell into disuse when births ceased to take place in private houses and moved to hospitals, under medical supervision. This happened not only in Minorca but in many places geographically and culturally far removed, and even in places with a different religion.

8. See T. Szasz *Ceremonial Chemistry* (New York 1974); I. Illich *Medical Nemesis* (London 1975); also L. Schwartzenberg and P. Viansson-Ponté *Changer la Mort* (Paris 1977) pp. 125-32.

Sebastian Brock

The Syrian Baptismal Rites

FORMATION PERIOD OF THE ANTIOCHENE TRADITION

THE ANTIOCHENE liturgical tradition is represented by four different rites, the Syrian Orthodox/Catholic, the East Syrian/Chaldean, the Maronite, and (previous to its Constantinopolitanisation in the early middle ages) the Melkite.[1] The formative period which produced the various baptismal services in more or less their present form was the fifth to seventh centuries. Although the East Syrian baptismal formulary stands somewhat apart from the others, the basic structure of all four rites is essentially the same, consisting of: 1. the initial ceremonies which originally belonged to the catechumenate (in the three West Syrian rites, but no longer in the East Syrian, these consist of inscription, exorcism, renunciation of Satan, greeting of Christ); 2. one or two pre-baptismal anointings, before and/or after the central prayer of consecration of the water; 3. baptism by immersion or affusion, using a passive formula ('N. is baptised . . .'); 4. post-baptismal anointing, with myron in the three West Syrian rites, but with oil in the East Syrian (sometimes this is replaced by an imposition of hands); 5. communion.

At an earlier stage of development (prior to the fifth century) there was only one anointing, which was pre-baptismal; originally this was of the forehead, but later it was extended to the whole body as well, thus sometimes giving rise to two separate pre-baptismal anointings. The post-baptismal anointing must have been first introduced into the Antiochene rite about AD 400, as the result of a number of different factors (the inner dynamic of the rite, the influence of practice at Jerusalem, the practice of anointing repentant schismatics and heretics). This background of the post-baptismal anointing makes any straight equation of it with western Confirmation very unsatisfactory and indeed positively misleading: what is important is that at all times in the history of the

Syrian baptismal rite there have been two essential constituent elements, anointing and baptism proper, irrespective of the order in which these elements occur.

In the course of the development of the Syrian rites a number of shifts of emphasis have taken place, and so it is necessary to consider the formative period in a little detail in order best to appreciate these rites in their present form.

In its original form the Syrian rite consisted essentially of a pre-baptismal anointing (of the forehead), called the *rushma* or 'mark', followed by baptism (normally immersion). The conceptual model for this structure was provided by the Jewish initiation rite of circumcision followed by proselyte baptism, and early Syriac writers are still very much aware that the pre-baptismal anointing, conferring the 'mark' of ownership, corresponds to, and at the same time replaces, circumcision, the mark of identity under the old covenant.

THE MEANING OF THIS TRADITION

Although in structure the Christian rite thus followed its Jewish model, its meaning and significance has been radically altered, thanks to the infusion of a whole number of new elements, all biblical in origin.

First and foremost, Christ's own baptism is seen as providing the fountainhead of Christian baptism, and here the most important element was the public proclamation of his Sonship (Mark 1:11 and parallels). Already in certain parts of the New Testament it seems that Christ's baptism was regarded as an 'anointing' (Acts 10:38; cf. Luke 4:18), and the choice of Psalm 2:7 provided basis for understanding Jesus' baptism as his public anointing as Messiah-King. Syrian tradition added to this the conferring of priesthood as well, through the hands of the Levite John the Baptist.

But besides serving as the public proclamation of his Sonship, Christ's baptism is understood in Syrian tradition as having a further dimension: His very presence in the Jordan 'purifies' and 'sanctifies' not only the Jordan waters, but also, in sacred time, all baptismal water: water, which in itself is an ambiguous element, capable of destruction as well as being the source of life, now takes on a new role, for by being sanctified it now becomes the potential means for the sanctification of mankind. This potential is then realised in each individual ceremony of Christian baptism at the invocation of the Holy Spirit which serves as the climax of the long prayer of consecration of the baptismal water.

But not only is Christian baptism thus ultimately dependent on Christ's baptism, it also confers on the Christian by grace what was Christ's by nature, for the Christian is reborn as a 'son of God', and he too has conferred upon him the royal priesthood (in its Syriac translation I Peter 2:9 reads: '. . . a chosen race, serving as priests for the Kingdom').

Now according to a strand of Old Testament tradition that was regarded as normative by both Jews and Christians, the conferring of both priesthood and kingship was by anointing, and in the Talmud it is specifically stated that this was in the form of the Greek letter *chi* (that is, a cross shape) on the forehead. There can be no doubt that this was the reason why the old 'mark' of circumcision in the Jewish initiation rite was replaced by the anointing on the forehead in its Christian counterpart.

The anointing and the baptism are thus intimately tied up with each other as far as the meaning of the early Syrian baptismal rite was concerned. Baptism was seen primarily as rebirth to something new (John 3); it is the conferring of a new mode of existence on the baptismal candidate, a mode of existence that had originally belonged to man before the Fall, but which had been lost at the Fall. Syriac writers are particularly fond of expressing this idea by means of the imagery (Jewish in origin) of the 'robe of glory', which Adam and Eve possessed in Paradise, but which had been lost at the Fall; Christ brings back the robe for mankind, and leaves it in the Jordan waters for mankind to put on again in baptism. Significantly this robe of glory which Adam wore in Paradise was already understood in Jewish tradition as being both priestly and royal. Baptism is thus regarded as the means of recovery of the proper relationship between man and God, in whose image he had been created.

Two points here will strike the western Christian at once: there is little or no hint in the early Syrian rite of the Pauline teaching of baptism as death, burial and rising with Christ (Romans 6); and the pre-baptismal anointing is essentially charismatic in character, in total contrast to the cathartic and exorcistic role that the pre-baptismal anointing has in other rites.

LATER DEVELOPMENTS

The end of the fourth century saw an important shift in conceptual models which was to have a profound influence on the structure and understanding of the Syrian rite: it was at this time that great prominence came to be given to the Pauline understanding of baptism as death and burial. Now if the font is seen as representing the grave, rather than a womb (following the older Syrian tradition), then there is no place for a pre-baptismal anointing of a charismatic character. It is basically this change of emphasis, the shift from Johannine to Pauline imagery, that resulted in the reinterpretation of the pre-baptismal anointing primarily as something cathartic and protective. Thus in late fourth-century writers such as John Chrysostom (who does not yet know a post-baptismal anointing) there is a strong tendency to concentrate all the positive benefits of the baptismal rite as a whole on to the baptism (even, ironically, the priesthood). It is significant, too, that at about the same time attention is focussed on the fact that at Christ's baptism the Holy Spirit descended upon Him *after* he had gone up from the Jordan waters. Everything thus pointed to the introduction of a new post-baptismal anointing in the Syrian rite to take over the role previously played by the pre-baptismal *rushma*.[2]

A study of the prayers and rubrics of the four Syrian rites as they emerged in the fifth to seventh centuries indicates that, although great emphasis is laid in the West Syrian rites on the new post-baptismal anointing with myron as the completing 'seal' of the Holy Spirit, the gifts of the Spirit originally associated with the *rushma* are mentioned, sometimes in connection with the new post-baptismal anointing, sometimes associated with the baptism, and sometimes still in the context of one of the two pre-baptismal anointings. The fact that several prayers are found now in one context, now in another, simply emphasises the great inconsistency that now reigns as a result of the shift in understanding and imagery that came about in the late fourth century: old and new are juxtaposed with scant regard for logic. The same situation can be seen in some of the early treatises on the myron (seventh century onwards): the myron is described, not only as conferring all the gifts of the Spirit originally associated with the pre-baptismal anointing, but also as having the protective and apotropaic character that the *rushma* only came to acquire at a secondary stage, with the introduction of the Pauline grave imagery.

Although from a strictly logical point of view the extant Syrian baptismal formularies thus present a rather bewildering and confused aspect to the eyes of the liturgical historian, nevertheless this state of affairs at the same time serves to emphasise the unity of the rite as a whole: anointings and baptism are inextricably mixed up, making the medieval western developments, with the separation off of Confirmation from Baptism, unthinkable.

RICHNESS OF SYMBOLISM

It is important at the same time, to look at the positive side: what we have in the Syrian rites as they come down to us is an accumulation of imagery resulting in an extraordinary richness of symbolism and meaning. Moreover, the interrelationship between individual elements in the rites and the rites as a whole is such that any attempt to isolate and attach specific meaning exclusively to one or other element in the rites is to misunderstand the essentially Semitic mentality out of which the Syrian formularies arose: we are not dealing with a series of logical steps, each readily distinguishable, but with a fluid network of symbols and imagery, where each element is enhanced by its relationship to what precedes and to what follows. It is a case of profusion, not of confusion.

This may be illustrated in two different ways. It has already been seen how the earliest Syrian tradition concentrated primarily on Christ's own baptism as a model. This does not mean that this tradition ignored the importance of Christ's death and resurrection in salvation history: the neglect is only apparent, not real, for the effects of the Incarnation as a whole are seen as being focussed on the particular moment of Christ's baptism; the fact that the Passion and Resurrection had not then yet taken place in historical time is irrelevant, for in sacred time, which is operative in all liturgy, the Nativity, Baptism, Passion and Resurrection all come together as a single unit, and as such can be located at any relevant point in the incarnate life of Christ. This understanding is expressed in the Syrian rites in a number of different ways, but perhaps nowhere more clearly than in a Syrian Orthodox prayer which speaks of the three focal 'staging posts' of the Incarnation—the womb of Mary, the womb of the Jordan, and the womb of Sheol. Also of great importance in this connection is the typological use made of John 19:34, where the water and blood from the side of Christ are regularly understood as referring to baptismal water and the Eucharist.[3] As the epiclesis in a prayer common to the three West Syrian rites puts it: 'May your Holy Spirit come and reside upon this water, sanctify it and make it like the water which flowed from the side of your Only-Begotten on the cross'.

If we turn now to the rich imagery of the Syrian rites,[4] we find the same sort of situation. What to the logical mind appears as sheer contradiction is really nothing of the sort: the paradox, for example, of the font being described both as a womb and as a grave (such as we find in many formularies) is by no means a straight-forward contradiction, but rather the paradox serves to transcend the two opposites and hint at a *tertium quid* which lies beyond the means of rational human description.

Finally we may survey rapidly some of the main ways in which the Syrian tradition speaks of the gifts of the Spirit at baptism.

First and foremost it is 'sonship' which the Holy Spirit confers at baptism: the baptised becomes a brother or sister to Christ and is now authorised to address God as Father, and so to use the 'our Father' (a prayer forbidden to catechumens). Since it is the indwelling of the Holy Spirit which allows the Christian to address God as Father (Romans 8:15), the gift of sonship implies the gift of the Spirit Himself.

Becoming a 'son of God' is closely associated with becoming a 'limb' or 'member' of Christ's mystical body, His Church. As a matter of fact this particular Pauline imagery is not as prominent in Syrian tradition as the related imagery of the baptised as lambs branded with the 'mark' of Christ in the flock of Christ the Shepherd who Himself became a Lamb to be slaughtered on behalf of His sheep.

As we have seen, the baptised are frequently described as putting on the 'robe of glory' (cf. Isaiah 61:3; sometimes also 'of light' or 'of the Spirit') at baptism, and this is associated primarily with the investiture of the baptismal candidate with the royal priesthood. This imagery, together with the typological use of John 19:34, can be said to be two distinctive hall-marks of Syrian tradition; both see baptism in terms of a return to Paradise, but this Paradise is not only the primordial paradise of Genesis, it is also the eschatological paradise of the Kingdom. The Christian is given the potential to enter this eschatological paradise at his baptism, and thus he possesses the 'pledge' of the Kingdom; to realise, already on earth, this potential entry into the Kingdom is the whole aim of the Christian life, and this is seen as a process of continual purification and sanctification (above all with the help of the Sacraments) culminating in the actual divinisation of man. This last idea, in fact characteristic of Eastern Christianity in general, is not openly expressed in the baptismal formularies themselves, but is found in Syriac writers from the fourth century onwards; as the greatest of all Syriac poets, St Ephrem (died 373), put it:

> The Son has made beautiful the servant's deformity
> and he has become a god, just as he desired.
>
> (Hymns on Virginity, 48:18).

CONCLUSION

The Syrian liturgical tradition represents the opposite pole to some western developments where economy of language (laudable in itself) has sometimes led to a dry reductionism. In the Syrian churches liturgy is very much an expression of symbolic theology; it is thus only to be expected that the baptismal formularies themselves, as well as the commentaries, should witness to an outstandingly rich theology of baptism—a theology that at the same time is profoundly rooted in the Bible.

Notes

1. The most accessible translation (into Latin) of the main *ordines* is in H. Denzinger *Ritus Orientalium* I, (Würzburg 1863). For further bibliographical details see my 'The Syriac baptismal ordines, with special reference to the anointings' *Studia Liturgica* 13 (1978).

2. See G. Winkler 'The Original Meaning of the Prebaptismal Anointing and its Implications' *Worship* 52, 1 (1978) pp. 24-45, and my 'The transition to a Post-baptismal anointing in the antiochene rite' to appear in the *Festchrift for A. H. Couratin* (Leiden 1978).

3. See my 'The mysteries hidden in the side of Christ' *Sebornost* 7, 5 (1978).

4. A detailed study is given in my *The Holy Spirit in the Syrian Baptismal Tradition*, Syrian Churches Series 9 (Kerala 1978) (forthcoming).

Contributors

WILLEM BERGER was born in 1919 at Utrecht and ordained a priest in 1944. He has been curate for six years and studied psychology. He has published articles in *Theologie en Pastoraat* and *Tijdschrift voor Pastorale Psychologie,* both of which periodicals he edits. He lectures in religious psychology and pastoral psychology at the Catholic University of Nijmegen.

AD BLIJLEVENS, CSSR, who was born in 1930 in Made-Drimmelen in the Netherlands, is professor of liturgy and spirituality in the Faculty of Theology and Pastorate at Heerlen.

HENRI BOURGEOIS was born in 1934 in Roanne (France). He is a Catholic priest. He studied theology, philosophy and psychology at the Institut Catholique in Lyons and at the Sorbonne in Paris. He is at present teaching theology and anthropology at the Institut Pastoral and in the Faculty of Theology in Lyons. He is also a director of religious education in Lyons and a member of a national team in charge of religious education in France. His publications include *Mais il y a le Dieu de Jésus Christ* (Paris 1970), *Libérer Jésus. Christologies actuelles* (Paris 1977).

SEBASTIAN BROCK is lecturer in Aramaic and Syriac in the University of Oxford, and a Fellow of Wolfson College. He is the author of numerous articles on the Syrian baptismal rites; his books include *The Harp of the Spirit: Twelve Poems of the St Ephrem* (London 1975) and *The Holy Spirit in the Syrian Baptismal Tradition* (Kerala 1978) (forthcoming).

SALVADOR CARDUS was born in Terrassa (Barcelona) in 1954, holds a Licentiate in Sociology from the University of Barcelona, and has specialised in research into the sociology of religion. His articles have appeared in several sociological journals.

MICHEL DUJARIER was born in Tours (France) in 1932. He received his doctorate in theology in 1962. A priest of *Fidei Donum,* he has been a parish priest in the diocese of Cotonou (Benin) since 1961. He is an instructor at the Catholic Institute of West Africa at Abidjan, and secretary of the Catechetic and Liturgical Commission for French-speaking West Africa. With A. Laurentin he has published *Catéchumenat: Données de l'histoire et perspectives nouvelles* (Paris 1969), and is a regular contributor to several journals.

JOAN ESTRUCH, born in Barcelona in 1943, studied at the universities of Barcelona and Louvain. A Licentiate in Philosophy and Literature and a Doctor of Sociology, he lectures in sociology at Barcelona University and is director of a research centre dealing with the sociology of religion. His published works include *Los protestantes españoles* (Barcelona 1968; Paris 1969), and *La secularización en España* (Bilbao 1972), as well as many articles on the sociology of religion.

ADRIEN NOCENT, OSB, was born in 1913. He taught for ten years at the Lumen Vitae Institute in Brussels. He has been a professor at San Anselmo since its foundation in 1961. He has published numerous articles and has contributed to several symposia. His books include *The Liturgical Year* in four volumes. His edition of the *Sacrementaire de Angoulême* (with F. Dell'Oro) will be published soon.

ABEL PASQUIER is a White Father who was born in 1932 at Petite-Boissière, France and ordained priest in 1959. He has a degree in theology (Gregorianum) and a doctorate in sociology (Paris). He has done pastoral work in the Upper Volta, followed by teaching at the Institut Supérieur d'Abidjan (Ivory Coast). At present he teaches in the department of Theology and Religious Sciences at the Institut Catholique in Paris. He has published accounts of his field studies as well as articles on catechetics.

ANTHONIUS SCHEER was born in 1934, at Kampen, Holland and ordained priest in 1959. He specialised in liturgiology at San Anselmo and at the Institut Supérieur de Liturgie, Paris. He is an adviser on the National Council for Liturgy and since 1976 has been lecturing at the Catholic University of Nijmegen.

LUIGI DELLA TORRE was born in 1927 in Pizzighettone (Cremona, Italy) and was ordained in 1952. A graduate of the University of Milan in mathematics and physics, he has been rector of a seminary (Ascoli Piceno), taught pastoral liturgy at San Anselmo and, from 1969 to 1975, been a parish priest in Rome. At present he is co-editor of *Servizio della Parola* and of the *Rivista di Pastorale Liturgica*. He has published many books and articles on liturgy, catechetics and adult education.

JAN VAN DER LANS was born in 1933 in the Hague. He has studied and practised psychology as well as philosophy and theology. He is a member of the Council of the psychological sector of the Faculty and of the council and research committee of the Faculty of Theology in the University of Nijmegen.

GIORGIO ZEVINI, SDB, was born in 1939 at Castelgandolpho (Rome) and ordained in 1968. He has degrees in Biblical Theology and Holy Scripture. He is at present lecturer in New Testament exegesis at the Salesian Pontifical University in Rome, and has published several books on his speciality.

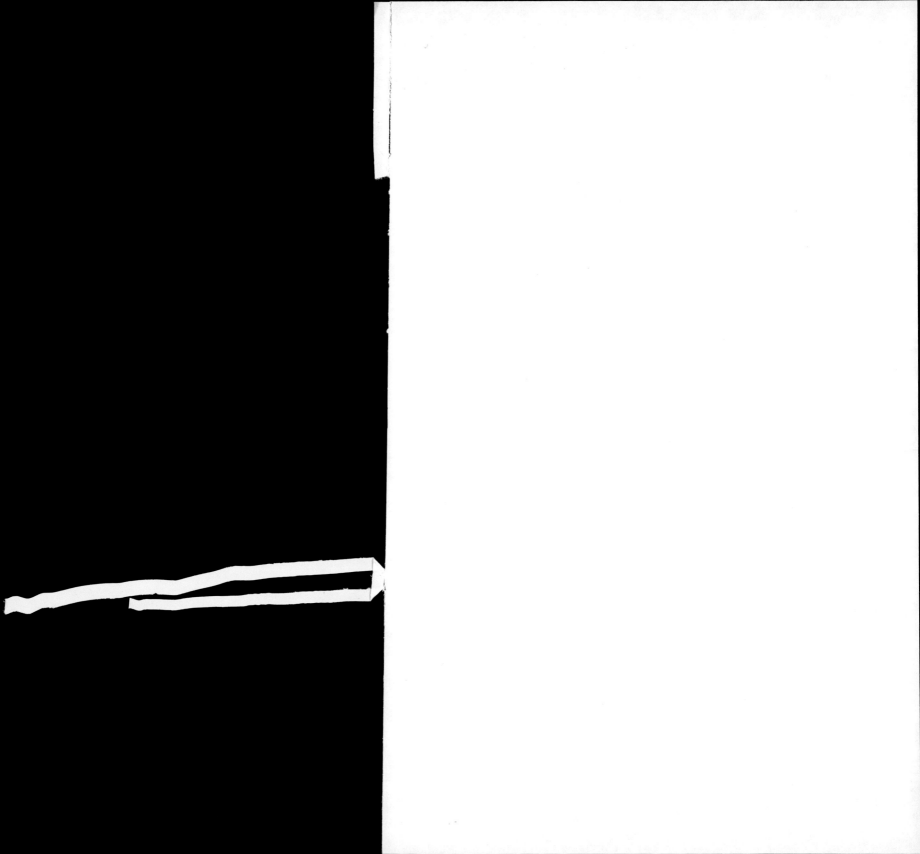

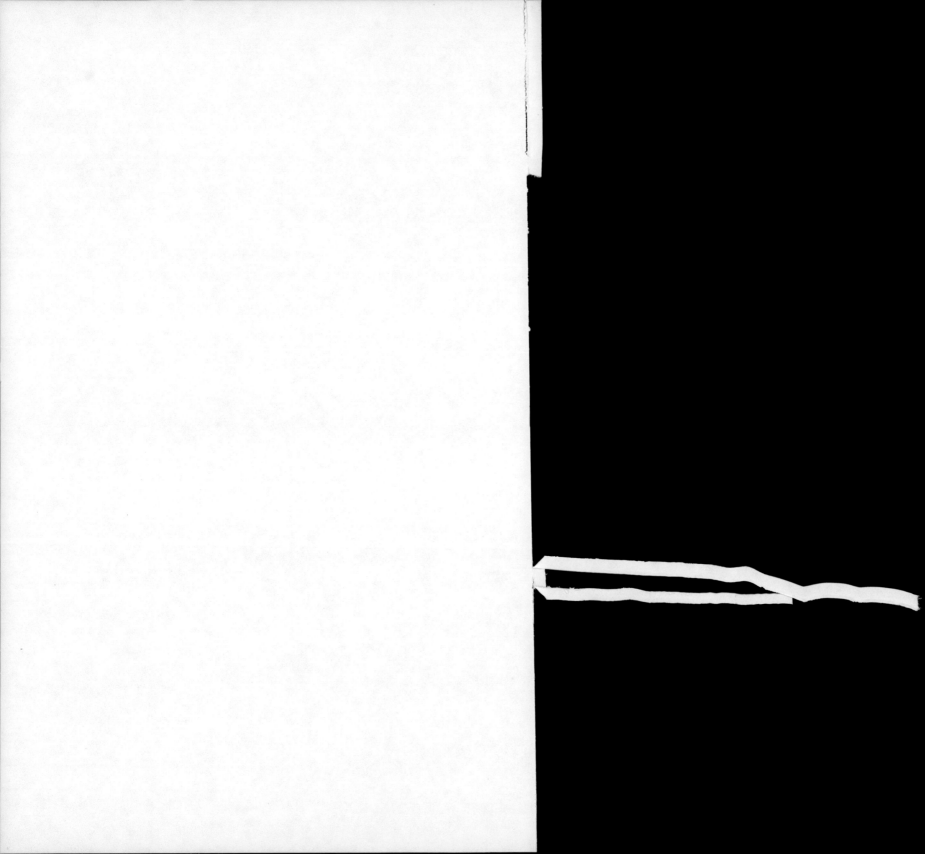

DATE DUE

NOV 25 '89			
JAN 5 '90			
OCT 20 1996			
MAR 0 7 2001			